Art In The Workplace

Fostering Creativity and Innovation

Neil J Milliner

Books by Neil J Milliner

BOOKS BY
NEIL J MILLINER

For Jodi DiLiberto—
the artist whose vision colors my world.

Your creativity is a reminder that art is not just something we make,
but something we live. Your courage, your curiosity, and the way you
transform emotion into color continue to inspire every page I write.

To anyone holding this book:
If you wish to see the heart behind my own creative life, visit Jodi's work
at From the Purple House:
www.fromthepurplehouse.art

Her art is a world of its own—vibrant, intuitive, and deeply human.
I'm endlessly grateful to walk beside her.

Contents

Perceptions

Art in the Workplace

Fostering Creativity and Innovation

DISCLAIMER:

The publisher and the author make no guarantees concerning the level of success you may experience by following the advice and strategies contained in this book, and you accept the risk that results will differ for each individual. The testimonials and examples provided in this book show results, which may not apply to the average reader, and are not intended to represent or guarantee that you will achieve the same or similar results.

The publisher and the author do not make any guarantee or other promise as to any results that may be obtained from using the content of this book. You should never make any investment decision without first consulting with your own financial advisor and conducting your own research and due diligence. To the maximum extent permitted by law, the publisher and the author disclaim any and all liability in the event any information, commentary, analysis, opinions, advice and/ or recommendations contained in this book prove to be inaccurate, incomplete or unreliable, or result in any investment or other losses.

Artful Valuation: How Corporate Art Collections Elevate Commercial Property Values

The Hidden Treasures Within Corporate Walls

Welcome to the world of corporate art collections, where the walls of commercial spaces transform into galleries of inspiration and innovation. In "Artful Valuation," we unravel the often-overlooked connection between corporate art and property values, exploring how a thoughtfully curated collection can elevate the overall worth of commercial real estate.

"The Business of Aesthetics: Crafting an Artful Corporate Identity"

In "The Business of Aesthetics," we delve into the role of art in shaping a distinct corporate identity. Explore how the visual appeal of a well-curated art collection resonates with clients, employees, and investors, creating a unique brand image that contributes to the overall perceived value of the commercial property.

"Beyond the Boardroom: Art as a Productivity and Wellbeing Catalyst"

"Beyond the Boardroom" explores the impact of art on productivity and employee wellbeing. Discover how strategically placed artworks can enhance the work environment, fostering creativity, reducing stress, and contributing to a positive corporate culture. Uncover the correlation between a thriving workforce and increased property value.

"Investing in Inspiration: The Artful Appeal to Clients and Investors"

"Investing in Inspiration" dives into the ways in which corporate art collections serve as a powerful tool for client engagement and investor attraction. Explore case studies and examples of businesses that have successfully leveraged their art investments to create a captivating narrative, ultimately enhancing the perceived value of their commercial properties.

"Cultural Currency: The Role of Art in Community Engagement"

"Cultural Currency" examines how corporate art collections contribute to community engagement. From public art installations to partnerships with local artists, understand how businesses can become cultural hubs, positively influencing the local community. Explore the link between community connections and heightened property values in the commercial real estate landscape.

"Appraising Art: The Tangible Impact on Property Valuation"

"Appraising Art" takes a closer look at the tangible impact of corporate art collections on property valuation. Explore the methodologies used in appraising art and how these valuations translate into increased property values. Understand the financial significance of investing in art as a long-term strategy for commercial property owners.

"Future-Proofing Investments: Navigating Trends in Corporate Art Collections"

"Future-Proofing Investments" offers insights into navigating trends in corporate art collections. Explore how staying attuned to art market trends and evolving corporate values can ensure that the art investments continue to contribute positively to commercial property values over time. Gain a strategic perspective on aligning art curation with the ever-changing demands of the market.

Retail Renaissance: Elevating Shopping Experiences with Artful Wall Decor

The Artful Shopping Journey - Where Wall Decor Meets Retail Therapy

Step into the world of "Retail Renaissance," where the canvas of retail spaces transforms into a vibrant gallery of artful wall decor, creating an immersive shopping experience. In this exploration, we unravel the profound impact that carefully curated and strategically placed wall art can have on customer emotions, behavior, and, ultimately, sales. From the psychology of color to the storytelling power of murals, discover how artful wall decor is not just an aesthetic addition but a powerful tool for boosting sales in the retail realm.

The Visual Storefront - Inviting Shoppers with Artful Window Displays

In "The Visual Storefront," we delve into the importance of artful window displays as the first impression a store makes on potential customers. These displays are not just about showcasing products; they serve as an introduction to the store's personality and style. The section explores how well-designed and visually appealing window art captures the attention of passersby, inviting them to step into a world where their shopping journey begins with a dose of artistic allure.

The transformative power of the visual storefront lies in its ability to set the tone for the entire shopping experience. When artful window displays create a sense of curiosity and excitement, they entice potential customers to enter the store with a positive mindset. Retailers recognize that the visual storefront isn't just about displaying merchandise; it's about making a memorable and enticing first impression that paves the way for increased foot traffic and potential sales.

The Psychology of Color - Influencing Emotions and Buying Behavior

Explore "The Psychology of Color," where we unravel the impact of hues on customer emotions and buying decisions. This section delves into the art and science of color selection for retail spaces, discussing how certain colors evoke specific emotions and influence shoppers' perceptions. From calming blues to vibrant reds, discover how strategic color choices in wall decor can create an atmosphere that encourages longer stays, positive experiences, and ultimately, increased sales.

The transformative power of the psychology of color lies in its ability to tap into the subconscious minds of shoppers. When retailers use colors that align with the desired shopping experience, it can influence customers' moods and perceptions. Businesses recognize that the psychology of color isn't just about aesthetics; it's a strategic tool for shaping the overall shopping environment and creating a positive emotional connection with customers.

Navigating Store Layouts - Guiding Shoppers with Artful Signage

In "Navigating Store Layouts," we explore how artful signage and wall decor can play a crucial role in guiding shoppers through the retail space. This section discusses the importance of clear and visually appealing signage that enhances wayfinding and directs customers to key areas of interest. From mural-like navigation to strategically placed art installations, discover how effective store layouts can not only improve the shopping experience but also increase the likelihood of customers making unplanned purchases.

The transformative power of navigating store layouts lies in their ability to create a seamless and enjoyable journey for shoppers. When retailers use artful signage to guide customers through the store, it reduces confusion, enhances the overall experience, and encourages exploration. Businesses recognize that navigating store layouts isn't just about providing directions; it's about creating a well-orchestrated shopping adventure that keeps customers engaged and leads to increased sales.

Storytelling Murals - Crafting Narratives that Connect with Customers

Step into "Storytelling Murals," where we explore the narrative power of large-scale wall art in retail spaces. This section discusses how murals can tell a brand's story, create a unique atmosphere, and establish a connection with customers. From intricate designs that reflect the brand's ethos to interactive murals that invite customer participation, discover how storytelling murals go beyond mere decoration, becoming powerful tools for fostering emotional engagement and driving sales.

The transformative power of storytelling murals lies in their ability to turn retail spaces into immersive environments that captivate and resonate with customers. When businesses use murals to convey their brand identity and values, it creates a memorable and personalized experience for shoppers. Retailers recognize that storytelling murals aren't just about adding visual interest; they're about forging a deeper emotional connection that can lead to increased brand loyalty and, ultimately, sales.

Seasonal Sensations - Adapting Wall Decor to Capture Holiday Spirit

In "Seasonal Sensations," we explore the strategic use of wall decor to capture the spirit of holidays and seasons. This section discusses how retailers can adapt their wall art to align with seasonal themes, festivities, and trends. From festive displays during the holiday season to fresh, spring-inspired decor, discover how the flexibility of wall art allows retailers to stay relevant and create a sense of urgency and excitement that drives seasonal sales.

The transformative power of seasonal sensations lies in their ability to create a dynamic and ever-changing shopping environment. When retailers adapt their wall decor to reflect current seasons and holidays, it not only keeps the store visually interesting but also taps into the psychology of urgency and novelty. Businesses recognize that seasonal sensations aren't just about decoration; they're about leveraging the power of time-sensitive themes to boost customer engagement and drive seasonal sales.

Creating Instagrammable Moments - Turning Customers into Brand Ambassadors

Conclude our exploration with "Creating Instagrammable Moments," where we discuss how artful wall decor can turn customers into brand ambassadors through social media. This section explores how retailers can strategically design spaces that encourage customers to capture and share their shopping experiences on platforms like Instagram. Discover how turning the retail space into a backdrop for shareable moments not only enhances brand visibility but also creates a community of loyal customers who actively promote the brand.

The transformative power of creating Instagrammable moments lies in its ability to leverage the influence of social media in driving brand awareness and sales. When retailers design spaces that are visually compelling and shareable, it encourages customers to become part of the brand story. Businesses recognize that creating Instagrammable moments isn't just about aesthetics; it's about turning customers into valuable advocates who can significantly impact brand reach and, ultimately, drive sales.

Pixels and Palettes: Mastering the Art of Tech-Infused Office Decor

A Canvas of Connectivity - The Fusion of Art and Technology in the Workplace

Welcome to a world where pixels meet palettes, and technology seamlessly integrates with art to redefine office decor. In this exploration of "Pixels and Palettes," we unravel the artful tech integration that is reshaping office spaces. From interactive screens to digital displays, discover how the marriage of art and technology creates a dynamic and visually stimulating work environment that fosters creativity, collaboration, and a futuristic vibe.

Interactive Infusions - Transforming Walls into Dynamic Canvases

In "Interactive Infusions," we dive into the transformative power of turning office walls into dynamic canvases through interactive screens and displays. Forget about static wallpapers; businesses are embracing interactive technologies that allow employees to engage with digital art. From touch-sensitive screens that respond to gestures to interactive projections that turn meetings into collaborative art sessions, the integration of interactive tech not only enhances visual aesthetics but also fosters a culture of creativity and innovation.

The transformative power of interactive infusions lies in their ability to turn office walls into dynamic hubs of collaboration. When employees can interact with digital art in real-time, it adds an element of playfulness to the workplace. Businesses recognize that this infusion of interactivity isn't just about aesthetics; it's about creating a workspace where technology is a tool for both productivity and creative expression.

Dynamic Digital Signage - Elevating Corporate Communication

Explore "Dynamic Digital Signage," where we unravel how businesses are using digital displays for corporate communication and aesthetic enhancement. Instead of traditional static signage, companies are opting for dynamic displays that can be updated in real-time. From vibrant welcome screens in lobbies to digital notice boards in common areas, dynamic digital signage not only conveys information efficiently but also adds a modern and visually appealing touch to the corporate environment.

The transformative power of dynamic digital signage lies in its ability to streamline communication and enhance the overall aesthetic of the workspace. When information is presented in a visually engaging manner, it captures the attention of employees and visitors alike. Businesses recognize that this shift from static to dynamic communication isn't just about conveying messages; it's about creating an immersive and tech-savvy corporate culture.

Ambient Tech Lighting - Illuminating Spaces with Futuristic Brilliance

Step into "Ambient Tech Lighting," where we explore how

businesses are using futuristic lighting technologies to illuminate office spaces. From LED strips that change colors to smart lighting systems that respond to environmental factors, ambient tech lighting not only enhances visibility but also adds a layer of sophistication to the workplace. Imagine a workspace where the lighting adapts to the time of day, creating a seamless transition from natural to artificial light, promoting a healthy and productive work environment.

The transformative power of ambient tech lighting lies in its ability to create dynamic atmospheres that adapt to the needs of employees. When lighting is no longer static but responds to the dynamics of the workspace, it contributes to the overall wellbeing of individuals. Businesses recognize that this integration of ambient tech lighting isn't just about aesthetics; it's about fostering a workplace where technology enhances the comfort and productivity of employees.

Tech Murals and Projection Mapping - Artistry Unleashed

In "Tech Murals and Projection Mapping," we delve into the artful integration of technology to create immersive visual experiences. Imagine entire walls transforming into digital murals that change with the seasons or projection mapping that turns ordinary spaces into extraordinary canvases. This fusion of artistry and technology not only elevates the visual appeal of the office but also provides businesses with a versatile platform to convey brand messages, celebrate achievements, and inspire creativity.

The transformative power of tech murals and projection mapping lies in their ability to turn ordinary office spaces into immersive and inspiring environments. When technology becomes a tool for artistic expression, it adds a layer of innovation and dynamism to the workplace. Businesses recognize that this integration of tech and art isn't just about decoration; it's about creating an office space that sparks imagination and fuels the creative spirit.

Augmented Reality Workstations - Redefining the Employee Experience

Explore "Augmented Reality Workstations," where we uncover how businesses are leveraging augmented reality (AR) to redefine the employee experience. Instead of traditional workstations, companies are incorporating AR technologies that allow employees to interact with digital elements in their physical workspace. From customizable digital desktops to virtual collaboration spaces, augmented reality workstations not only enhance productivity but also create a futuristic and personalized work environment.

The transformative power of augmented reality workstations lies in their ability to blend the physical and digital realms seamlessly. When employees can customize their workspaces with digital elements and collaborate in virtual spaces, it adds a layer of personalization and flexibility to the work experience. Businesses recognize that this integration of AR isn't just about efficiency; it's about creating a workspace where technology adapts to the needs and preferences of individual employees.

Gamifying Break Areas - Playful Tech Integration for Employee Wellbeing

Conclude our exploration with "Gamifying Break Areas," where we unravel how businesses are using playful tech integration to enhance employee wellbeing in break spaces. From interactive games projected on walls to digital art installations that respond to movement, these tech-infused break areas not only provide a refreshing escape but also contribute to stress relief and team bonding. The integration of gaming elements in break areas adds a touch of playfulness to the workplace, fostering a positive and enjoyable atmosphere.

The transformative power of gamifying break areas lies in its ability to create moments of relaxation and connection for employees. When break spaces are infused with playful tech elements, it adds an element of fun to the workday, contributing to overall job satisfaction and wellbeing. Businesses recognize that this integration of gaming tech isn't just about entertainment; it's about creating a workplace where breaks become rejuvenating experiences.

Brand Consistency: Ensuring Your Wall Art Aligns with Company Messaging

Welcome to a visual journey where brand identity meets artistic expression - "Brand Consistency: Ensuring Your Wall Art Aligns with Company Messaging." In this exploration, we'll dive into the intricate dance between corporate messaging and wall art, uncovering the artful balance that ensures a seamless integration of visual aesthetics and brand values.

Setting the Canvas: The Role of Wall Art in Corporate Spaces

In "Setting the Canvas," we embark on an understanding of the foundational role wall art plays in corporate spaces. From lobbies to office corridors, discover how the right choice of art can set the tone for the entire workspace. Dive into the nuances of selecting pieces that not only resonate with the company's messaging but also create a welcoming and inspiring environment for employees, clients, and visitors.

Consider incorporating large-scale artworks that mirror the ethos of your brand, creating a visually cohesive and engaging atmosphere.

Visual Vocabulary: Translating Messaging into Artistic Elements

In "Visual Vocabulary," we delve into the process of translating company messaging into artistic elements. Explore how the visual language of your brand, including colors, symbols, and values, can be seamlessly woven into custom artworks. From murals that narrate the brand story to sculptures embodying core values, discover how these visual elements become a tangible representation of your company's identity.

Consider collaborating with artists who specialize in interpreting brand narratives into visual stories, ensuring a harmonious fusion of messaging and art.

The Power of Color: Evoking Emotions and Aligning with Brand Identity

In "The Power of Color," we unravel the psychology behind color choices in wall art and their profound impact on brand perception. Explore how specific colors can evoke emotions, aligning seamlessly with your brand's identity. From vibrant and energetic hues to calming and sophisticated tones, discover the strategic use of color in wall art to reinforce and amplify your company messaging.

Consider conducting a thorough analysis of your brand's color palette and incorporating these hues strategically into the selected artworks.

Narrative Continuity: Telling a Cohesive Story through Art Installations

In "Narrative Continuity," we explore the concept of using art installations to tell a cohesive story that aligns with your company messaging. Discover how a series of artworks strategically placed throughout the office can create a visual narrative that reinforces brand values and missions. From entrance installations to thematic displays, explore how narrative continuity in wall art can leave a lasting impression on employees and clients alike.

Consider commissioning artists to create a series of interconnected artworks that together tell a story, creating a dynamic and immersive experience.

Employee Connection: Fostering Brand Loyalty through Art in Workspaces

In "Employee Connection," we examine the role of wall art in fostering a sense of connection and loyalty among employees. Discover how personalized and relatable art in individual workspaces can contribute to a positive company culture. From employee-contributed art projects to personalized prints, explore the impact of creating a workspace that resonates with the individuals who bring your brand to life every day.

Consider involving employees in the selection or creation of artworks for their workspaces, fostering a sense of ownership and connection.

Adaptability and Change: Evolving Wall Art with Shifting Messaging

In "Adaptability and Change," we confront the challenge of evolving wall art to align with shifting company messaging. Explore how businesses can adapt their visual language to reflect changes in brand identity, values, or mission. From seasonal updates to reflecting current social or cultural movements, discover the flexibility required to ensure your wall art remains a dynamic and relevant extension of your company's messaging.

Consider establishing a periodic review process for wall art, allowing for updates and adaptations that align with the evolving nature of your brand.

Conclusion:

In "Brand Consistency: Ensuring Your Wall Art Aligns with Company Messaging," we've uncovered the artful synergy between visual aesthetics and brand values. From setting the canvas to translating messaging into artistic elements, harnessing the power of color, ensuring narrative continuity, fostering employee connection, and adapting to change, wall art emerges as a dynamic and integral component of brand consistency in corporate spaces.

Artful Collaboration: Bridging Business and Community Through Local Art in Corporate Spaces

The Canvas of Collaboration - Redefining Corporate Spaces with Local Art

Welcome to the vibrant intersection of "Artful Collaboration," where the worlds of business and community converge in a celebration of local art. In this exploration, we'll uncover the transformative power of incorporating local artwork into corporate spaces. From enriching office aesthetics to fostering community engagement, discover how businesses are redefining their environments and contributing to the vitality of the communities they inhabit.

Brushstrokes of Identity - The Impact of Local Art on Corporate Culture

In "Brushstrokes of Identity," we delve into the profound impact local art has on shaping corporate culture. Businesses are recognizing that the art adorning their walls isn't just decoration; it's a mirror reflecting the essence of the community. Local artists infuse their creations with the spirit, stories, and identity of the region, creating a unique tapestry that resonates with employees and visitors alike. This infusion of local identity fosters a sense of belonging and pride among employees, transforming the corporate space into a canvas that tells a story beyond the balance sheets and business strategies.

The transformative power of these brushstrokes lies in their ability to humanize the corporate environment. When employees are surrounded by art that speaks to their shared experiences and community, it bridges the gap between work and personal identity. Businesses recognize that this infusion of local identity isn't just about aesthetics; it's about cultivating a corporate culture that embraces and celebrates the diversity and richness of the community.

Nurturing Creativity - Local Art as a Catalyst for Innovation

Explore "Nurturing Creativity," where we uncover how local art serves as a catalyst for innovation within corporate spaces. The dynamic and diverse perspectives embedded in local artwork stimulate creativity and inspire fresh thinking among employees. Whether it's a sculpture in the lobby, a mural in the breakout area, or rotating exhibitions showcasing local talent, businesses are transforming their spaces into incubators of innovation. Local artists, with their unique interpretations of the world, challenge traditional mindsets and ignite the creative spark necessary for navigating the complex landscapes of modern business.

The transformative power of nurturing creativity lies in its ability to propel businesses toward innovation and adaptability. When employees are exposed to a spectrum of artistic expressions, it fosters a culture that values diverse perspectives and out-of-the-box thinking. Businesses recognize that this investment in creativity isn't just about aesthetics; it's a strategic move to stay agile and ahead in an ever-evolving business landscape.

Community Engagement - Artful Contributions Beyond Business Walls

In "Community Engagement," we explore how businesses are extending their influence beyond office walls to actively contribute to the cultural vibrancy of their neighborhoods. By featuring local artists in corporate spaces, businesses become patrons of the arts, supporting community talent and providing artists with exposure to a broader audience. This symbiotic relationship enriches the local arts scene while positioning the business as a dynamic and socially responsible entity.

The transformative power of community engagement lies in its ability to create meaningful connections beyond the business-consumer relationship. When businesses actively support local artists, they become integral parts of the community fabric, contributing to the cultural and economic well-being of the neighborhoods they call home. Businesses recognize that this commitment to community engagement isn't just a philanthropic gesture; it's a strategic move that builds trust and loyalty among local stakeholders.

Artful Workspaces - Enhancing Employee Well-Being and Productivity

Step into "Artful Workspaces," where we explore the role of local art in enhancing employee well-being and productivity. Beyond mere decoration, local artwork has the power to create environments that inspire and invigorate. Businesses are strategically incorporating art into workspaces, recognizing its impact on reducing stress, fostering creativity, and improving overall job satisfaction. Whether it's a calming mural in a breakout area, sculptures in communal spaces, or rotating exhibitions in meeting rooms, businesses are redefining their spaces to prioritize the holistic well-being of their employees.

The transformative power of artful workspaces lies in their ability to create environments where employees thrive, both personally and professionally. When employees work in surroundings that stimulate their senses and evoke positive emotions, it contributes to a more vibrant and productive workplace. Businesses recognize that this investment in employee well-being isn't just a perk; it's a strategic move that pays dividends in employee satisfaction, retention, and ultimately, the bottom line.

Economic Impact - Local Art as a Driver of Economic Growth

In "Economic Impact," we examine how businesses supporting local artists contribute to the broader economic growth of their communities. By showcasing and investing in local talent, businesses play a pivotal role in establishing art as a thriving economic sector. The ripple effect extends to galleries, studios, and ancillary services, creating a robust ecosystem that attracts cultural tourism, fosters entrepreneurship, and enhances the overall economic vitality of the region.

The transformative power of this economic impact lies in its ability to position businesses as integral components of a thriving local economy. When businesses actively participate in the cultural and economic development of their communities, it creates a positive feedback loop that benefits everyone involved. Businesses recognize that this commitment isn't just about art; it's about being catalysts for economic growth and prosperity in the places they operate.

Sustaining the Artful Connection - Long-Term Partnerships and Strategies

Conclude our exploration with "Sustaining the Artful Connection," where we delve into the strategies and long-term partnerships that ensure the continued success of the collaboration between businesses and local artists. From curated art programs and artist-in-residence initiatives to community art events and collaborative projects, businesses are forging enduring connections that go beyond mere transactions. The emphasis is on creating a sustainable model that not only benefits both parties but also contributes to the cultural legacy of the community.

The transformative power of sustaining the artful connection lies in its ability to build enduring relationships that withstand the test of time. When businesses and local artists engage in long-term partnerships, it goes beyond a one-time display; it becomes a narrative of shared growth, mutual support, and lasting impact. Businesses recognize that this sustained commitment isn't just about art; it's about weaving an ongoing tapestry of collaboration and community enrichment.

Custom Corporate Art: Tailoring Pieces to Reflect Company Values

Welcome to a world where the essence of a company is translated onto canvas – "Custom Corporate Art." In this blog post, we'll explore the profound impact of bespoke artworks in corporate spaces, unraveling the story of how custom pieces can serve as visual expressions of company values. From boardrooms to communal areas, discover the unique ability of tailored art to embody the ethos of a company and foster a positive and inspiring work environment.

The Art of Identity: Establishing Brand Presence

In "The Art of Identity," we delve into the significance of establishing brand presence through custom corporate art. Explore how companies are harnessing the power of art to visually communicate their identity. From large-scale installations in lobbies to signature pieces in reception areas, discover how customized artworks serve as silent ambassadors, leaving a lasting impression on clients, employees, and visitors.

Consider commissioning artworks that incorporate the company's logo, color palette, and key symbols, creating a cohesive visual identity throughout the office space.

Inspiration in the Boardroom: Fostering Creativity and Innovation

In "Inspiration in the Boardroom," we explore the role of custom corporate art in fostering creativity and innovation during critical decision-making moments. Discover how bespoke art installations in boardrooms contribute to a dynamic and inspiring atmosphere. From thought-provoking sculptures to interactive pieces, explore how these custom creations stimulate fresh perspectives and innovative thinking among company leaders.

Consider collaborating with local artists to create rotating installations that keep the boardroom environment dynamic and ever-evolving.

Expressing Values Through Art: Ethical and Social Responsibility

In "Expressing Values Through Art," we unravel the powerful connection between corporate values and customized artworks. Explore how companies are using art to express their commitment to ethical and social responsibility. From murals depicting philanthropic initiatives to sculptures symbolizing environmental sustainability, discover how art becomes a visual testament to a company's dedication to making a positive impact.

Consider hosting art events or exhibitions within the office space that highlight the company's social responsibility efforts, creating awareness among employees and visitors.

Employee Engagement: Custom Art in Shared Spaces

In "Employee Engagement," we examine the impact of custom corporate art in shared spaces, promoting a sense of unity and pride among employees. Explore how communal areas, such as break rooms and hallways, become canvases for expressing the collective spirit of a company. From team-building art projects to murals that celebrate diversity, discover how these customized artworks contribute to a positive and inclusive workplace culture.

Consider organizing art workshops or team-building activities that involve employees in the creation of custom art pieces, fostering a sense of ownership and collaboration.

Personalized Workstations: Art at the Desk Level

In "Personalized Workstations," we explore the concept of extending custom art to individual workspaces. Discover how companies are recognizing the value of personalized art at the desk level, allowing employees to surround themselves with pieces that resonate with their individual values and preferences. From custom prints to desk sculptures, explore how this approach enhances employee satisfaction and well-being.

Consider creating a program that allows employees to choose or contribute to the design of artworks for their individual workstations, promoting a personalized and empowering work environment.

Celebrating Milestones: Art as a Marker of Achievement

In "Celebrating Milestones," we delve into the tradition of using custom corporate art as a marker of achievement and success. Explore how companies commemorate significant milestones, anniversaries, or achievements through commissioned artworks. From dedicated walls showcasing historical achievements to specially crafted sculptures, discover how art becomes a visual narrative of a company's journey and success.

Consider collaborating with artists to create a series of artworks that celebrate specific milestones, fostering a sense of pride and motivation among employees.

Conclusion:

In "Custom Corporate Art: Tailoring Pieces to Reflect Company Values," we've explored the myriad ways in which bespoke artworks can be strategically integrated into corporate spaces. From establishing brand identity to fostering innovation, expressing values, engaging employees, personalizing workspaces, and celebrating achievements, custom corporate art emerges as a powerful tool for creating a visually captivating and emotionally resonant work environment.

Customer-Facing Spaces: How Wall Art Influences Client Perceptions

Step into the world of "Customer-Facing Spaces," where aesthetics meet client impressions. In this blog post, we explore the profound impact that well-curated wall art can have on client perceptions. From creating a welcoming atmosphere to conveying brand identity, discover how art transforms your customer-facing spaces into memorable experiences.

The Art of First Impressions: Crafting Welcoming Entrances

In "The Art of First Impressions," unravel the secrets of crafting inviting entrances through strategic wall art. Explore how the selection of colors, textures, and themes influences the initial perception of your space, setting the tone for positive client interactions. Learn about the psychology behind creating welcoming environments that leave a lasting impression.

Consider incorporating statement pieces or interactive installations near entrances to captivate clients from the moment they step through the door.

Brand Storytelling on Walls: Conveying Identity and Values

Dive into "Brand Storytelling on Walls" and understand the pivotal role art plays in conveying your company's identity. Explore the use of branded artwork, corporate colors, and visual elements that narrate the story of your brand. Delve into case studies highlighting successful implementations of brand storytelling through wall art in various industries.

Consider collaborating with local artists or graphic designers to create bespoke pieces that align with your brand's values and resonate with your target audience.

The Psychology of Colors: Influencing

Emotions and Decisions

Explore "The Psychology of Colors" and how the color palette of your wall art can evoke specific emotions in clients. Uncover the science behind color psychology and its influence on consumer behavior. From calming blues to energizing reds, discover the power of colors in shaping the overall mood of your customer-facing spaces.

Consider conducting research or surveys to understand the color preferences of your target demographic, ensuring your wall art resonates with your client base.

Artful Ambiance: Enhancing Client Comfort and Engagement

In "Artful Ambiance," discover the role of wall art in creating comfortable and engaging customer environments. Explore how the strategic placement of artwork can enhance the overall ambiance, encouraging clients to spend more time in your spaces. Learn about the balance between visual stimulation and tranquility for optimal client experiences.

Consider incorporating comfortable seating areas surrounded by visually appealing art to encourage clients to linger and engage with your brand.

Interactive Installations: Fostering Client Engagement and Connection

Dive into "Interactive Installations" and explore the exciting realm of hands-on client experiences through wall art. From touch-sensitive displays to augmented reality features, discover how interactive installations captivate clients, fostering a sense of connection and engagement. Learn about successful implementations and the positive impact on customer satisfaction.

Consider creating interactive displays that provide valuable information about your products or services, turning client interactions into memorable experiences.

Evolving Spaces: Rotating Art to Keep Things Fresh

In our final section, "Evolving Spaces," explore the concept of rotating wall art to keep customer-facing areas dynamic and fresh. Learn how regularly updating your art installations can prevent visual monotony, keeping clients intrigued and excited about each visit. Discover practical tips for seamlessly incorporating seasonal or themed rotations.

Consider establishing a schedule for art rotations, aligning them with key events, seasons, or promotions to maintain a sense of novelty in your customer-facing spaces.

Conclusion:

In "Customer-Facing Spaces: How Wall Art Influences Client Perceptions," we've unveiled the transformative potential of wall art in shaping the client experience. Elevate your spaces to leave an indelible mark on clients, creating environments that not only reflect your brand but also foster positive relationships. Transform your customer-facing spaces into showcases of artful expression, ensuring that every client interaction is a memorable one.

Customer-Centric Spaces: How Art Influences the Customer Journey

Embark on a captivating exploration of the symbiotic relationship between art and customer-centric spaces. In "Customer-Centric Spaces: How Art Influences the Customer Journey," we unravel the transformative power of artistic expressions in shaping memorable and engaging experiences for patrons.

Artful Entrances: Crafting First Impressions

In "Artful Entrances," we delve into the significance of crafting unforgettable first impressions through strategically placed art. Explore how businesses can curate welcoming entrances that captivate and set the tone for a positive customer journey. Discover the psychology behind artful entrances and how they contribute to a lasting impact on customers.

Consider implementing bold and thought-provoking art pieces at your entrance to create a visually stunning introduction, leaving a lasting impression on your customers.

Navigating Emotions: The Impact of Art on Customer Feelings

In "Navigating Emotions," we explore the profound influence of art on customer emotions. Delve into the psychology of color, form, and subject matter in evoking specific feelings and moods. Uncover how businesses can use art to create a harmonious and emotionally resonant environment, enhancing the overall customer experience.

Consider curating art that aligns with your brand's emotional tone, ensuring that each piece contributes positively to the emotional journey of your customers within your space.

Brand Storytelling Through Art: Connecting with Customers

In "Brand Storytelling Through Art," we unravel the storytelling potential of art in building connections with customers. Explore how businesses can use art to narrate their brand story, values, and mission. Witness the impact of art in creating a cohesive and authentic narrative that resonates with customers, fostering a sense of connection and loyalty.

Consider incorporating art installations that visually communicate your brand's story, creating a cohesive and memorable experience for your customers.

Personalized Spaces: Tailoring Art Experiences for Individual Customers

In "Personalized Spaces," we delve into the concept of tailoring art experiences for individual customers. Explore the role of data-driven personalization in curating art displays that cater to the diverse preferences of your customer base. Witness how personalized art experiences contribute to a sense of exclusivity and make customers feel truly understood.

Consider leveraging customer data to customize art displays, ensuring that each customer's journey is enriched by a unique and personalized artistic experience.

Interactive Art: Engaging Customers in the Creative Process

In "Interactive Art," we explore the dynamic world of customer engagement through participatory art experiences. Delve into the benefits of incorporating interactive art installations that invite customers to become active participants in the creative process. Witness how fostering creativity enhances the overall customer journey and encourages a sense of ownership.

Consider incorporating interactive art installations that invite customers to engage with and contribute to the artistic ambiance of your space, fostering a sense of community and collaboration.

Memorable Exits: Leaving a Lasting Impression

In "Memorable Exits," we conclude our journey by exploring the often overlooked aspect of the customer journey – the exit. Discover how businesses can create memorable exits by strategically placing impactful art near exit points. Explore the role of art in leaving customers with a positive and lasting impression, ensuring that their overall journey is one they'll fondly remember.

Consider curating art near exit points that encourages customers to reflect on their experience and leaves them with a positive and memorable impression as they leave your space.

Conclusion:

In the realm of "Customer-Centric Spaces: How Art Influences the Customer Journey," we've navigated the multifaceted impact of art on every stage of the customer experience. From artful entrances and navigating emotions to brand storytelling, personalized spaces, interactive art, and memorable exits, the integration of art in customer-centric spaces is an art form in itself. As businesses embrace the transformative potential of art, they elevate the customer journey into a dynamic and immersive experience that goes beyond transactions, fostering lasting connections.

Expressing Company Culture: The Role of Wall Art in Workplace Atmosphere

Step into the dynamic world of corporate aesthetics, where the walls of your office become a canvas to express the heartbeat of your company. In this blog post, we embark on a journey through the intricacies of "Expressing Company Culture" and the pivotal role that wall art plays in shaping the very atmosphere of your workplace.

1. Setting the Tone: The Impact of Entryway Art

Our exploration begins with "Setting the Tone," emphasizing the crucial role of entryway art. Dive into the significance of the first visual encounter employees and visitors experience. Discover how carefully selected pieces can set the stage for the company's ethos, leaving a lasting impression that echoes throughout the workspace.

Consider incorporating elements of your company's mission statement or core values into the entryway art for a powerful visual representation.

2. Collaborative Corners: Art in Shared Workspaces

In "Collaborative Corners," we navigate the shared spaces where employees collaborate and ideate. Explore how strategically placed art can fuel creativity and encourage teamwork. From vibrant murals to interactive installations, learn how to cultivate an environment where the walls themselves inspire collaboration and a sense of community.

Consider involving employees in the selection or creation of artwork for shared spaces, fostering a collective sense of ownership.

3. Desks with a View: Personalizing Workstations with Art

Our third section, "Desks with a View," focuses on the impact of personalizing individual workstations. Dive into the idea that art isn't confined to common areas but extends to each employee's desk. Discover how allowing employees to curate their workspace with art that resonates with them can enhance job satisfaction and contribute to a positive work atmosphere.

Consider organizing periodic art rotations to keep individual workspaces dynamic and reflective of evolving employee interests.

4. Company Values on Display: Art in Meeting Rooms

"Company Values on Display" delves into the significance of art in meeting rooms. Explore how strategic art choices can visually reinforce company values during important discussions and decision-making processes. From motivational pieces to subtle nods to company milestones, learn how art in meeting rooms can communicate a strong sense of identity and purpose.

Consider commissioning custom artwork that aligns with the themes of your company's values and goals.

5. Celebrating Milestones: Art as a Chronicle of Achievements

In our penultimate section, "Celebrating Milestones," we uncover the power of art to chronicle a company's journey. Delve into the idea of using walls as a canvas for commemorating achievements, anniversaries, and milestones. Learn how a visual timeline can not only tell the story of your company but also inspire employees with a sense of pride and shared accomplishments.

Consider creating a designated wall space specifically for showcasing company milestones and accomplishments.

6. *Sustainability in Art: Reflecting Ethical Values in Decor*

Our final exploration, "Sustainability in Art," addresses the importance of reflecting ethical values in workplace decor. Dive into the world of eco-friendly and sustainable art choices that not only express your commitment to ethical practices but also contribute to a positive workplace atmosphere aligned with contemporary values.

Consider implementing a company-wide initiative to support local artists and environmentally conscious art options.

Conclusion:

In "Expressing Company Culture: The Role of Wall Art in Workplace Atmosphere," we've delved into the nuanced ways art shapes the ambiance of your workplace. From entryways to individual workstations, each section of this blog post serves as a guide to curating an environment that vibrantly expresses your company's culture, fostering a positive and inspiring workspace.

Artful Valuation: How Corporate Art Collections Elevate Commercial Property Values

The Hidden Treasures Within Corporate Walls

Welcome to the world of corporate art collections, where the walls of commercial spaces transform into galleries of inspiration and innovation. In "Artful Valuation," we unravel the often-overlooked connection between corporate art and property values, exploring how a thoughtfully curated collection can elevate the overall worth of commercial real estate.

"The Business of Aesthetics: Crafting an Artful Corporate Identity"

In "The Business of Aesthetics," we delve into the role of art in shaping a distinct corporate identity. Explore how the visual appeal of a well-curated art collection resonates with clients, employees, and investors, creating a unique brand image that contributes to the overall perceived value of the commercial property.

"Beyond the Boardroom: Art as a Productivity and Wellbeing Catalyst"

"Beyond the Boardroom" explores the impact of art on productivity and employee wellbeing. Discover how strategically placed artworks can enhance the work environment, fostering creativity, reducing stress, and contributing to a positive corporate culture. Uncover the correlation between a thriving workforce and increased property value.

"Investing in Inspiration: The Artful Appeal to Clients and Investors"

"Investing in Inspiration" dives into the ways in which corporate art collections serve as a powerful tool for client engagement and investor attraction. Explore case studies and examples of businesses that have successfully leveraged their art investments to create a captivating narrative, ultimately enhancing the perceived value of their commercial properties.

"Cultural Currency: The Role of Art in Community Engagement"

"Cultural Currency" examines how corporate art collections contribute to community engagement. From public art installations to partnerships with local artists, understand how businesses can become cultural hubs, positively influencing the local community. Explore the link between community connections and heightened property values in the commercial real estate landscape.

"Appraising Art: The Tangible Impact on Property Valuation"

"Appraising Art" takes a closer look at the tangible impact of corporate art collections on property valuation.

Explore the methodologies used in appraising art and how these valuations translate into increased property values. Understand the financial significance of investing in art as a long-term strategy for commercial property owners.

"Future-Proofing Investments: Navigating Trends in Corporate Art Collections"

"Future-Proofing Investments" offers insights into navigating trends in corporate art collections. Explore how staying attuned to art market trends and evolving corporate values can ensure that the art investments continue to contribute positively to commercial property values over time. Gain a strategic perspective on aligning art curation with the ever-changing demands of the market.

Safeguarding Masterpieces: A Comprehensive Guide to Navigating Art Insurance

In the captivating world of art, protecting your investments goes beyond mere brushstrokes and aesthetics. Art insurance emerges as a guardian of your cherished masterpieces, offering a shield against unforeseen circumstances. In this guide, we'll navigate the intricacies of art insurance with a friendly tone, ensuring that you embark on this journey with confidence and clarity.

1: Art Insurance Unveiled: Understanding the Basics

Before delving into the specifics, it's essential to grasp the fundamental principles of art insurance. This section provides a friendly introduction, breaking down the basics of what art insurance is and why it's a crucial component of responsible art ownership. From protecting against theft and damage to considering coverage for transit and storage, understanding the foundational aspects lays the groundwork for a secure art collection.

Transitioning seamlessly from the canvas to the insurance realm, art enthusiasts and collectors alike will find this section a valuable starting point in demystifying the world of art insurance.

2: Appraisal Adventures: Determining

the Value of Your Art

The first step in securing art insurance is understanding the value of your collection. This section guides you through the appraisal process, demystifying the intricacies of determining the worth of your artworks. Friendly tips on working with professional appraisers, keeping accurate records, and staying informed about market trends ensure that you embark on your appraisal adventure armed with knowledge and confidence.

Just as an artist carefully crafts each stroke, meticulous attention to detail in the appraisal process sets the stage for comprehensive and accurate art insurance coverage.

3: Tailoring Coverage: Customizing Insurance to Your Collection

Every art collection is as unique as the individual pieces it comprises. This section explores the art of tailoring insurance coverage to suit the specific needs of your collection. From considering the type of art you own to understanding the nuances of different insurance policies, we delve into the friendly intricacies of customizing coverage.

Navigating the insurance landscape becomes an empowering experience as you learn to ask the right questions, ensuring that your coverage aligns with the distinctive character of your art investments.

4: The Quest for the Right Insurer: Choosing Your Art Insurance Partner

Much like selecting the perfect frame for a painting, choosing the right insurer is a critical decision in the art insurance journey. This section provides a friendly guide to the quest for the ideal insurance partner, offering tips on researching reputable insurers, understanding policy terms, and evaluating customer reviews.

With a friendly tone, we navigate the landscape of insurance providers, empowering you to make an informed decision that aligns seamlessly with your art protection needs.

5: Art in Transit: Safeguarding Your Collection on the Move

Whether you're transporting artworks to exhibitions, galleries, or a new home, safeguarding your collection in transit is paramount. This section explores the friendly art of ensuring comprehensive coverage during transportation. From understanding the risks associated with transit to exploring insurance options specifically tailored for art on the move, we guide you through the intricacies of safeguarding your masterpieces on their journey.

Transitioning seamlessly from the stationary gallery to the mobile canvas, this section ensures that your art remains protected and cherished, even when on the move.

6: The Claim Chronicles: Navigating the Art Insurance Claim Process

In the unfortunate event that you need to make a claim, navigating the process with ease is essential. This section offers a friendly guide to the claim chronicles, walking you through the steps of filing a claim, documenting damage, and liaising with your insurer. Understanding the claim process ensures that, in times of adversity, you can navigate the journey with confidence and efficiency.

Just as an artist learns from experience, this section empowers you with the knowledge to confidently navigate the claim process, turning potential challenges into manageable steps toward restoration and recovery.

Educational Spaces: Inspiring Learning with Engaging Wall Art

Welcome to "Educational Spaces: Inspiring Learning with Engaging Wall Art," where we embark on a journey to explore the dynamic relationship between art and education. From vibrant classrooms to stimulating libraries, discover how thoughtfully curated wall art can transform educational spaces into inspiring environments that foster creativity and a love for learning.

The Art of Learning: Cultivating Creativity in Classrooms

In "The Art of Learning," we dive into the heart of education – the classroom. Explore how vibrant and engaging wall art can enhance the learning experience, creating a stimulating environment that encourages curiosity and creativity. Learn about the impact of visual aesthetics on student engagement and discover creative ways to integrate educational themes into the classroom decor.

Consider incorporating interactive and educational wall art to make your classroom an inspiring space for both educators and students.

Literary Landscapes: Bringing Stories to Life in Libraries

In "Literary Landscapes," we turn our attention to libraries as sanctuaries of knowledge and imagination. Uncover the power of storytelling through wall art and how it can transport library visitors to different worlds. Explore the role of murals, quotes, and literary-themed art in creating an atmosphere that sparks a passion for reading and lifelong learning.

Consider transforming your library with captivating wall art that celebrates the magic of literature and invites readers into captivating realms.

Historical Murals: Journeying Through Time in Educational Spaces

Embark on a historical voyage in "Historical Murals" as we explore the impact of visualizing history through art. Learn how educational spaces can be enriched with murals depicting historical events, figures, and timelines. Discover the potential of historical wall art in fostering a deeper understanding and appreciation for the past, creating immersive learning experiences.

Consider incorporating historical murals into classrooms and corridors, transforming educational spaces into captivating time machines.

STEM Spectacles: Infusing Science and Technology into Art

In "STEM Spectacles," we bridge the gap between science, technology, engineering, and mathematics (STEM) and the world of art. Explore how educational spaces can benefit from STEM-inspired wall art, making complex concepts visually accessible and engaging. Learn about the synergy between creativity and critical thinking in fostering well-rounded, innovative thinkers.

Consider integrating STEM-themed art installations to inspire the next generation of scientists, engineers, and creative problem solvers.

Motivational Corners: Nurturing Ambition with Inspirational Art

Discover the impact of motivation in "Motivational Corners" and the role of inspirational wall art in shaping positive attitudes. Explore how carefully curated motivational quotes, success stories, and goal-oriented visuals can transform corners of educational spaces into motivational hubs. Learn about the psychology of motivation and its contribution to creating a conducive learning environment.

Consider dedicating spaces within educational institutions to motivational corners adorned with empowering wall art.

Interactive Learning Walls: Engaging Minds Through Creativity

In "Interactive Learning Walls," we explore the innovative fusion of technology and art to create interactive educational experiences. Discover how digital and augmented reality art installations can bring subjects to life, providing students with hands-on and immersive learning opportunities. Explore the potential of interactive learning walls in promoting collaboration, creativity, and a deeper understanding of academic content.

Consider embracing interactive learning walls as a modern approach to education, encouraging students to engage with subjects in dynamic and meaningful ways.

Conclusion:

In "Educational Spaces: Inspiring Learning with Engaging Wall Art," we've unraveled the profound impact of art in transforming classrooms, libraries, and educational environments into dynamic spaces that nurture creativity and inspire a love for learning. By integrating thoughtful and engaging wall art, educational spaces can become more than places of instruction—they can become hubs of inspiration, innovation, and lifelong curiosity.

Harmony Unveiled: Mastering Feng Shui with Wall Art for Positive Energy Flow

Step into a world where ancient wisdom meets contemporary aesthetics as we explore the union of Feng Shui and wall art. In this blog post, "Harmony Unveiled," we'll delve into the transformative power of art in enhancing the energy flow within your home. From creating serene havens of tranquility to fostering spaces of vitality and creativity, join us on a journey through the art of Feng Shui and discover how your walls can become conduits of positive energy.

The Art of Placement: Arranging Wall Art for Chi Circulation

Embark on our journey with "The Art of Placement," where we unravel the essence of Feng Shui in arranging wall art for optimal chi circulation. Consider the Bagua map, a Feng Shui tool that divides your space into nine areas, each representing a different aspect of life. Explore how specific wall art placements within these areas can influence the flow of energy and enhance corresponding aspects of your life.

Whether it's placing serene landscapes in the Health and Family area or vibrant abstracts in the Creativity and Fame zone, the art of placement goes beyond mere aesthetics. It becomes a deliberate act of channeling positive energy throughout your home. Uncover the secrets of arranging your wall art to invite harmony and balance into every corner.

Elemental Balance: Infusing Five Elements into Your Wall Art

Transition into "Elemental Balance," where we explore the infusion of the five elements—Wood, Fire, Earth, Metal, and Water—into your wall art. In Feng Shui, each element corresponds to specific aspects of life and carries its own energy. Discover how selecting art that represents or complements these elements creates a harmonious balance, fostering a dynamic flow of energy within your space.

Consider incorporating wooden frames for the Wood element, fiery red hues for Fire, or metallic finishes for Metal. The elemental balance in your wall art not only adds visual interest but also aligns with the principles of Feng Shui, promoting a sense of equilibrium and vitality. Immerse yourself in the art of elemental infusion and witness the transformative energy it brings.

Color Magic: Harnessing Feng Shui Colors for Positive Vibes

In the third section, "Color Magic," we explore the profound impact of Feng Shui colors in wall art on the energy of your living space. Each color carries its own energy and symbolism, influencing the atmosphere and emotions within a room. Dive into the world of color psychology within Feng Shui, from calming blues and greens to energizing reds and yellows.

Consider selecting wall art that aligns with the desired energy for a particular room. A tranquil bedroom may benefit from serene blues, while a lively living room could thrive with the vibrancy of reds and oranges. Discover how harnessing Feng Shui colors in your wall art choices creates a visually appealing and energetically charged environment that resonates with positivity.

Reflective Wisdom: Mirrors and Art for Expanding Space and Energy

Move on to "Reflective Wisdom," where we explore the strategic use of mirrors in conjunction with wall art to expand both physical space and energy. Mirrors in Feng Shui are known for their ability to amplify energy and reflect light, creating a sense of openness and abundance. When strategically combined with art, mirrors become powerful tools for enhancing the flow of positive chi.

Consider placing mirrors adjacent to wall art to visually expand the space and reflect the beauty of your chosen pieces. This combination not only brings depth to your decor but also magnifies the energetic impact of your art. Delve into the reflective wisdom of Feng Shui and discover how mirrors and art together can transform confined spaces into expansive havens.

Nature's Bounty: Integrating Natural Elements Through Wall Art

Enter the fifth section, "Nature's Bounty," where we explore the integration of natural elements in wall art to connect with the Earth's energy. Feng Shui emphasizes the importance of grounding and connecting with nature to enhance well-being. Discover how incorporating art featuring landscapes, flora, or fauna brings the rejuvenating essence of the outdoors into your indoor spaces.

Consider selecting wall art that resonates with your personal connection to nature, whether it's a serene beach scene, a lush forest, or botanical prints. This infusion of natural elements not only beautifies your walls but also infuses your home with the grounding energy of the Earth. Immerse yourself in the bounty of nature's embrace through carefully curated wall art.

Personalized Energy: Infusing Your Intentions into Custom Wall Art

In the final section, "Personalized Energy," we explore the transformative power of infusing your intentions and personal energy into custom wall art. Feng Shui encourages the intentional selection of art that resonates with your goals, aspirations, and the energy you wish to manifest in your life.

Consider collaborating with artists to create custom pieces that reflect your personal journey, values, or aspirations. Whether it's a vision board-style collage or a commissioned piece inspired by your intentions, personalized wall art becomes a tangible expression of your desires. Unleash the power of your personal energy into your living space through custom creations that align with the principles of Feng Shui.

Conclusion:

As we conclude our journey through the symbiotic relationship between Feng Shui and wall art, remember that each piece you choose has the potential to be more than just a decoration. It can be a conduit for positive energy, a source of inspiration, and a reflection of your intentions. Whether you're arranging art for chi circulation, infusing elemental balance, harnessing color magic, employing reflective wisdom, embracing nature's bounty, or personalizing your energy, the art of Feng Shui is an ongoing journey toward creating a harmonious and energized living space.

Business Renaissance: Revitalizing Spaces with Artistic Renewal

The Artful Revival of Business Spaces

Welcome to the "Business Renaissance," a journey where the infusion of art breathes new life into corporate environments. In this exploration, we delve into how businesses are undergoing a transformative revival, turning mundane spaces into vibrant, creative hubs. From boardrooms to break areas, discover the power of artistic renewal in sparking innovation, fostering employee well-being, and redefining the corporate ethos.

The Canvas of Creativity - Art in Corporate Lobbies

In "The Canvas of Creativity," we unravel how businesses are reimagining their lobbies as artistic gateways. This section explores the strategic use of sculptures, installations, and vibrant murals to welcome clients and employees alike. By transforming these entrance points into engaging art galleries, companies set the stage for a redefined corporate identity that communicates innovation and creativity.

The transformative power of the canvas of creativity lies in its ability to make a strong first impression, signaling to visitors and employees that this is not just a workspace but a dynamic hub of innovation. When businesses invest in artistic lobbies, it goes beyond aesthetics, creating an environment that speaks to the company's commitment to creativity and forward-thinking.

Meeting of Minds - Artful Boardrooms That Inspire

Step into "Meeting of Minds," where we explore the role of art in redefining corporate boardrooms. This section discusses how businesses are incorporating thought-provoking artwork, innovative designs, and interactive installations to transform traditional meeting spaces. Discover how artful boardrooms foster a collaborative atmosphere, inspire creativity, and enhance the overall quality of strategic discussions.

The transformative power of the meeting of minds lies in its ability to turn boardrooms into dynamic spaces that inspire innovation. When businesses infuse art into the heart of their decision-making environments, it communicates a commitment to creativity and a willingness to think outside the conventional corporate box. Companies recognize that the meeting room isn't just a place for discussions; it's a canvas for cultivating ideas and shaping the future.

Creative Corners - Nurturing Innovation in Break Areas

Explore "Creative Corners," where we uncover the growing trend of businesses creating artful break areas to foster innovation and employee well-being. This section delves into how companies are strategically placing sculptures, murals, and interactive art installations in break spaces, transforming them into vibrant hubs that recharge and inspire. Discover the impact of these creative corners on employee morale, collaboration, and overall workplace satisfaction.

The transformative power of creative corners lies in their ability to turn break areas into dynamic, rejuvenating spaces that contribute to employee happiness and productivity. When businesses prioritize art in these spaces, it communicates a commitment to nurturing creativity and well-being, recognizing that breaks are not just moments of rest but opportunities for inspiration and collaboration.

The Cubicle Canvas - Personalizing Workspaces with Art

In "The Cubicle Canvas," we explore how businesses are empowering employees by allowing them to personalize their workspaces with art. This section delves into the positive impact of allowing individuals to curate their surroundings, creating an environment that reflects their personality and inspires productivity. Discover how the cubicle canvas is transforming traditional workspaces into personalized havens that boost employee satisfaction and engagement.

The transformative power of the cubicle canvas lies in its ability to turn individual workspaces into reflections of identity and creativity. When businesses encourage employees to personalize their cubicles with art, it goes beyond mere decoration, creating a sense of ownership and pride. Companies recognize that the cubicle isn't just a workstation; it's a canvas for self-expression and a catalyst for individual and collective productivity.

Artful Leadership - Executive Offices That Inspire Vision

Step into "Artful Leadership," where we explore how businesses are reimagining executive offices as spaces that inspire visionary leadership. This section discusses the strategic use of art in the offices of top executives, transforming them into environments that reflect innovation, foresight, and corporate values. Discover how artful leadership spaces contribute to shaping the company's culture and communicating a forward-thinking vision.

The transformative power of artful leadership lies in its ability to turn executive offices into symbolic representations of a company's values and aspirations. When businesses invest in art for these spaces, it sends a powerful message about the importance of creativity and vision at the highest levels of leadership. Companies recognize that executive offices aren't just administrative spaces; they're canvases for inspiring and shaping the future direction of the business.

Employee-Curated Exhibits - Fostering a Collective Artistic Identity

Conclude our journey with "Employee-Curated Exhibits," where we explore the trend of businesses fostering a collective artistic identity by allowing employees to curate exhibits within the workplace. This section discusses the positive impact of empowering employees to contribute to the artistic expression of the company, creating a shared narrative that builds a sense of community and collaboration.

The transformative power of employee-curated exhibits lies in their ability to turn the workplace into a dynamic gallery of diverse voices and perspectives. When businesses embrace the idea of collective artistic expression, it fosters a sense of belonging and shared identity among employees. Companies recognize that the workplace isn't just a physical space; it's a canvas for the collective creativity of the entire team.

Canvas Capital: Artistic Trends in Real Estate - A Valuable Investment Strategy

The Brushstroke of Value in Real Estate

Welcome to the world where canvas meets capital, exploring the integration of artistic trends as a powerful investment strategy in real estate. In this guide, we unravel the secrets of leveraging art to enhance property value, offering insights into how embracing artistic trends can be a game-changer in the realm of real estate investment. Get ready to embark on a journey where aesthetics and assets seamlessly converge.

"Artful Architecture: The Impact of Art-Inspired Design on Property Value"

In "Artful Architecture," we delve into the impact of art-inspired design on property value. Explore how real estate developers and architects are incorporating artistic elements into their designs, creating visually stunning and unique properties. From avant-garde structures to buildings that mimic famous artworks, discover how artful architecture not only attracts attention but also elevates the perceived value of a property, making it a standout investment in a competitive market.

Witness the transformative power of artful architecture and

its influence on the valuation of real estate.

"Curating Value: The Role of Curated Art Collections in Property Enhancement"

In "Curating Value," we explore the rising trend of curated art collections within real estate spaces. Dive into the world of developers strategically curating art pieces to enhance the ambiance and allure of residential and commercial properties. Learn how a well-curated art collection can create a sense of exclusivity, turning a property into a unique investment opportunity. Discover the symbiotic relationship between curated art and property value, where aesthetics drive desirability and, in turn, enhance the investment potential.

Explore the art of curating value and witness how art collections contribute to the overall appeal of real estate.

"Smart Art Integration: The Intersection of Technology and Real Estate Investment"

In "Smart Art Integration," we explore the intersection of technology and real estate investment. Learn how developers are incorporating smart art installations to create immersive and interactive experiences within properties. Dive into the world of digital art, augmented reality, and smart home features that not only provide a modern and luxurious living experience but also contribute to the long-term value of a property. Discover how the marriage of art and technology is shaping the future of real estate investments.

Uncover the possibilities of smart art integration and its impact on the tech-savvy real estate market.

"Artful Neighborhoods: Community

Development and Property Values"

In "Artful Neighborhoods," we shift our focus to community development and its impact on property values. Explore how the integration of public art, cultural spaces, and community art initiatives can turn neighborhoods into desirable locations for real estate investment. Learn how the creation of artful communities not only enhances the quality of life for residents but also contributes to the appreciation of property values over time. Discover the ripple effect of artistic engagement on the overall appeal of a neighborhood and its real estate market.

Experience the transformative influence of artful neighborhoods and their role in shaping property values.

"The Art Investor's Dilemma: Navigating Trends for Long-Term Value"

In "The Art Investor's Dilemma," we navigate the complexities of art trends and their impact on long-term property value. Explore the delicate balance between embracing current artistic trends and ensuring enduring value in real estate investments. Learn how to navigate the evolving landscape of artistic preferences, understanding the fine line between trendy and timeless. Gain insights into making informed decisions as an art-focused real estate investor, maximizing the potential for sustained property appreciation.

Confront the art investor's dilemma and discover strategies for long-term value in the dynamic real estate market.

"Art-Infused ROI: The Financial Benefits of Investing in Artistic Real Estate"

In "Art-Infused ROI," we delve into the financial benefits of investing in artistic real estate. Explore case studies and success stories where artful investments have resulted in substantial returns. From increased property values to enhanced rental yields, discover the tangible financial advantages of integrating artistic elements into real estate portfolios. Uncover the potential for art-infused ROI and how strategic investments in creative spaces can yield both aesthetic and financial dividends.

Unlock the secrets of art-infused ROI and witness the financial benefits of investing in artistic real estate.

Artful Hospitality: Elevating the Guest Experience in Hotels and Resorts

The Canvas of Comfort

Welcome to the world of "Artful Hospitality," where the ambiance of hotels and resorts transforms into a masterpiece of guest experience. In this journey, we explore how the strategic integration of art elevates customer satisfaction, turning each stay into a memorable and immersive encounter. From lobby installations to in-room artwork, discover the transformative power of art in hospitality that goes beyond mere decoration.

The Welcome Palette - Artful Lobbies That Set the Tone

In "The Welcome Palette," we delve into the role of art in hotel lobbies, examining how the strategic placement of sculptures, paintings, and installations contributes to the overall guest experience. Explore how hotels use their lobbies as a canvas, setting the tone for the entire stay. From curated galleries to immersive installations, discover how artful lobbies create a welcoming and unforgettable first impression.

The transformative power of the welcome palette lies in its ability to establish a sense of identity for the hotel or resort. When guests are greeted by thoughtfully curated art, it goes beyond aesthetics, creating a unique atmosphere that resonates with the brand's essence. Hoteliers recognize that the lobby isn't just a transitional space; it's an opportunity to immerse guests in the hotel's story, making them feel not just accommodated but truly welcomed.

Room with a View - The Artful Ambiance of Guest Rooms

Step into "Room with a View," where we explore how hotels and resorts enhance guest rooms with carefully selected artwork. This section examines the impact of in-room art on the overall ambiance and guest satisfaction. From bespoke paintings to thematic decor, discover how hotels use art to create an immersive and personalized experience for every guest.

The transformative power of the room with a view lies in its ability to turn guest rooms into private galleries, offering a retreat that goes beyond comfort. When hotels invest in curated art for guest rooms, it adds a layer of sophistication and personalization, ensuring that each stay is a unique and memorable experience. Hoteliers recognize that guest rooms aren't just places to rest; they're canvases for creating a sense of sanctuary and luxury.

Culinary Canvases - Elevating Dining Experiences with Artful Spaces

Explore "Culinary Canvases," where we unravel how hotels and resorts use art to elevate dining experiences. This section discusses the strategic integration of art in restaurants, bars, and dining areas to create a multisensory experience for guests. From mural-adorned walls to immersive installations, discover how artful spaces enhance the overall enjoyment of culinary delights.

The transformative power of culinary canvases lies in their ability to turn dining into a sensorial journey, where art and gastronomy converge. When hotels create artful spaces for dining, it elevates the entire culinary experience, making it not just about the food but also the ambiance. Hoteliers recognize that culinary spaces aren't just venues for meals; they're stages for creating memorable and immersive dining adventures.

Nature's Artistry - Incorporating Landscapes and Outdoor Installations

In "Nature's Artistry," we explore how hotels and resorts embrace the natural canvas around them, integrating landscapes and outdoor art installations to enhance the guest experience. This section examines the use of gardens, sculptures, and outdoor artworks to create a harmonious connection between the built environment and nature. Discover how hotels leverage the beauty of outdoor spaces to provide guests with moments of tranquility and inspiration.

The transformative power of nature's artistry lies in its ability to create a seamless blend between the man-made and natural elements of a hotel or resort. When outdoor spaces are thoughtfully designed with artistic intent, it fosters a connection with nature, offering guests a rejuvenating and aesthetically pleasing environment. Hoteliers recognize that nature's artistry isn't just about landscaping; it's about creating holistic and immersive experiences that transcend the confines of the hotel.

Artful Experiences - Curated Events and Workshops for Guests

Step into "Artful Experiences," where we explore how hotels and resorts curate art events and workshops to engage and entertain guests. This section delves into the diverse range of activities, from art exhibitions to creative workshops, that hotels organize to provide guests with unique and enriching experiences during their stay. Discover how these artful initiatives contribute to guest satisfaction and the overall appeal of the hotel.

The transformative power of artful experiences lies in their ability to turn a hotel stay into a cultural and intellectual journey. When hotels go beyond traditional amenities and offer curated art events, it adds value to the guest experience, creating memorable moments that go beyond the typical hospitality offerings. Hoteliers recognize that artful experiences aren't just about accommodation; they're about providing guests with opportunities for exploration, learning, and cultural enrichment.

Artful Legacy - Supporting Local Artists and Communities

Conclude our exploration with "Artful Legacy," where we discuss the significance of hotels and resorts supporting local artists and communities. This section examines the positive impact of collaborations with local artists, art initiatives, and community engagement programs on both the hotel's brand and the surrounding community. Discover how hotels contribute to the cultural tapestry by fostering artistic talent and promoting a sense of shared responsibility.

The transformative power of artful legacy lies in its ability to create a lasting impact that extends beyond the confines of the hotel. When hotels actively support local artists and communities, it builds a legacy of cultural enrichment and social responsibility. Hoteliers recognize that artful legacy isn't just about individual success; it's about contributing to the broader cultural landscape and leaving a positive imprint on the communities they are a part of.

Canvas Connections: Nurturing Teamwork in Shared Art Spaces

The Palette of Team Collaboration

Dive into the vibrant world of canvas connections, where shared art spaces become the palette for nurturing teamwork. In this blog post, we unravel the transformative power of artful collaboration, exploring how shared creative environments foster team cohesion, communication, and innovation. Discover how the collective act of creating art transcends traditional team-building activities, laying the foundation for a more connected and collaborative workplace.

The Artful Icebreaker - Breaking Down Barriers Through Shared Creation

The journey begins with the artful icebreaker, a creative way to break down barriers and initiate team collaboration. Shared art spaces provide a neutral ground where team members can express themselves freely, fostering a sense of openness and camaraderie. Consider launching collaborative art projects that require input from every team member, such as a mural or a group sculpture. This not only encourages participation but also creates a shared experience that forms the basis for stronger connections.

The artful icebreaker goes beyond traditional team-building activities by tapping into the inherent creativity of individuals. It allows team members to see each other in a different light, fostering a deeper understanding and appreciation of diverse talents within the group. As the first strokes are applied to the canvas, the artful icebreaker sets the stage for a more collaborative and harmonious team dynamic.

Collaborative Canvases - Creating Shared Masterpieces

Enter the realm of collaborative canvases, where team members come together to create shared masterpieces. Providing a larger canvas—both metaphorically and literally —encourages collective ideation and problem-solving. Choose themes that resonate with the team's goals or current projects, turning the art creation process into a tangible reflection of the team's collective identity. Collaborative canvases are not just about the finished product; they are about the collaborative journey that leads to it.

Consider rotating the responsibility for leading different aspects of the art project, allowing each team member to take on a leadership role and contribute their unique skills. As the collaborative canvases evolve, they become visual representations of the team's collective creativity and problem-solving capabilities. This shared masterpiece becomes a source of pride and a reminder of what the team can achieve when working together.

Artistic Dialogue - Enhancing Communication Through Shared Art Spaces

Artistic dialogue emerges as a powerful tool for enhancing communication within teams. Shared art spaces create an environment where team members communicate not just verbally but also visually. Encourage the use of art as a language for expressing ideas, emotions, and even challenges. Consider incorporating regular art sessions or workshops where team members can visually communicate their thoughts, fostering a more inclusive and expressive form of dialogue.

Artistic dialogue allows team members to explore new ways of expressing themselves, breaking away from traditional communication barriers. The act of creating art together enhances active listening and understanding, creating a more empathetic team dynamic. As teams engage in artistic dialogue, they discover alternative channels for expressing complex ideas and emotions, ultimately strengthening their overall communication skills.

Fusion of Perspectives - Celebrating Diversity in Shared Art Spaces

The fusion of perspectives becomes a celebration of diversity in shared art spaces. Artistic collaboration provides a platform for team members to showcase their unique perspectives, experiences, and cultural influences. Consider incorporating themes that celebrate diversity or encourage team members to infuse elements from their backgrounds into the art projects. The fusion of perspectives not only adds richness to the artistic creations but also promotes a culture of appreciation and respect for individual differences.

Shared art spaces become a melting pot of ideas, where diverse perspectives converge to create something truly unique. This collaborative celebration of diversity goes beyond the artistic process; it becomes a valuable lesson in understanding, accepting, and embracing the richness that each team member brings to the table. The fusion of perspectives transforms shared art spaces into symbolic representations of unity within diversity.

Innovation on Canvas - Inspiring Creativity and Problem-Solving

Innovation on canvas unfolds as shared art spaces become incubators for creativity and problem-solving. Engaging in collaborative art projects challenges teams to think outside the box, experiment with unconventional ideas, and approach problem-solving in a non-linear manner. Consider introducing art sessions specifically designed to stimulate creativity and encourage teams to explore new ways of approaching challenges.

Artistic collaboration provides an outlet for innovation, allowing team members to experiment with different techniques, materials, and perspectives. The process of creating art together becomes a metaphor for the innovative process within the workplace. As teams navigate the artistic journey, they cultivate a mindset of exploration and risk-taking that can be applied to their professional endeavors, fostering a more innovative and adaptive team culture.

Beyond the Canvas - Translating Artful Collaboration into the Workplace

As the final stroke on the canvas of canvas connections, the focus turns to translating artful collaboration beyond the artistic space and into the workplace. Consider incorporating lessons learned from shared art spaces into everyday team activities and projects. Create opportunities for team members to continue collaborating and expressing themselves creatively within the workplace. By fostering a culture of artful collaboration, the impact of shared art spaces extends beyond individual projects and becomes a transformative force that shapes the overall team dynamic.

Encourage the continuation of collaborative art projects or the integration of artistic elements into the physical workspace. Whether it's a dedicated art wall, rotating exhibits of team-created art, or regular art sessions, the lessons learned from shared art spaces become an integral part of the team's ongoing collaboration and creative expression.

Art Consultation Services: Elevating our Space with Professional Expertise

The Art of Transformation - Unlocking the Potential of Your Space

Embark on a transformative journey as we explore the invaluable role of "Art Consultation Services" in enhancing the aesthetic appeal and market value of your property. Discover how professional advice can turn your space into a curated masterpiece, reflecting your personality and captivating potential buyers.

"Navigating the Artistic Landscape: The Need for Guidance"

In "Navigating the Artistic Landscape," we delve into the complexities of the art world and why seeking professional advice is crucial. Explore the myriad options available and how an art consultant can help you navigate the vast landscape, ensuring that every piece chosen aligns seamlessly with your vision and the property's character.

"Tailored Aesthetics: Customizing Art to Your Space"

Explore "Tailored Aesthetics" and understand how art consultation services go beyond generic recommendations. Dive into the process of customizing artworks to fit your space perfectly, considering factors like size, color schemes, and thematic elements that harmonize with your property's unique features.

"Budgeting Brilliance: Maximizing Impact Within Constraints"

In "Budgeting Brilliance," discover the art of maximizing impact within budget constraints. Uncover how art consultants excel in curating a collection that aligns with your financial parameters while ensuring each piece contributes significantly to the overall ambiance and aesthetic appeal.

"Strategic Placement: The Art of Spatial Harmony"

Explore "Strategic Placement" and learn how art consultants excel in the delicate art of spatial harmony. Delve into the significance of placing artworks thoughtfully, creating focal points that draw attention to your property's best features while enhancing the overall flow and ambiance.

Section 5: "Curation with Purpose: Enhancing the Property's Story"

In "Curation with Purpose," understand how art consultation services add a layer of narrative to your property. Discover the strategic curation that weaves a story, making your space more engaging and emotionally resonant for potential buyers, transforming it into a place they can envision calling home.

"The Investment Perspective: Art as a Property Asset"

Conclude our journey with "The Investment Perspective," exploring how art consultation services can enhance your property's overall value. Understand the long-term benefits of strategic art investments and how they contribute to the property's market appeal, making it a more attractive prospect for potential buyers.

Tradition and Modernity: Blending Art Styles in Traditional Businesses

Step into the harmonious intersection of heritage and innovation with our exploration of "Tradition and Modernity: Blending Art Styles in Traditional Businesses." In this captivating journey, we'll unravel the nuances of seamlessly merging classic and contemporary art forms within the context of traditional establishments.

Artful Entrances: Bridging Eras with Inviting Displays

In "Artful Entrances," we explore the pivotal role of the first impression in traditional businesses. Discover how strategically combining classic and modern art at the entrance sets the tone for a unique experience. Dive into the art of creating welcoming spaces that honor tradition while embracing the freshness of contemporary aesthetics.

Consider incorporating a curated display at the entrance that features a blend of traditional art pieces and modern installations, creating a visual symphony that captivates visitors.

Cultural Fusion: Infusing Local Heritage with Global Perspectives

In "Cultural Fusion," we delve into the rich tapestry of blending local traditions with global perspectives through art. Explore how businesses can celebrate their cultural roots while incorporating modern artistic expressions. Witness the powerful impact of this fusion in creating an inclusive and eclectic atmosphere that resonates with diverse audiences.

Consider curating art displays that showcase the local heritage alongside contemporary interpretations, fostering a connection between the traditional and the global.

Nostalgic Narratives: Storytelling Through Art Installations

In "Nostalgic Narratives," we uncover the storytelling potential of art installations within traditional businesses. Explore how carefully selected artworks can narrate the history, values, and milestones of a business. Witness the transformative power of nostalgic narratives in creating an emotional bond with customers, who become part of the ongoing story.

Consider incorporating art installations that serve as visual chronicles, allowing customers to immerse themselves in the rich history and narrative of your traditional establishment.

Functional Art: Traditional Forms in Modern Applications

In "Functional Art," we explore the innovative use of traditional art forms in modern applications within traditional businesses. Dive into examples of businesses seamlessly integrating classic craftsmanship into functional elements, creating an environment where tradition is not just celebrated but actively contributes to the daily operations.

Consider incorporating handcrafted traditional elements into functional aspects of your business, such as custom-made furniture, signage, or even packaging, adding a touch of authenticity to every interaction.

Modernizing Spaces: Revitalizing Interiors

with Contemporary Art

In "Modernizing Spaces," we take a closer look at the transformative effect of infusing contemporary art into the interiors of traditional establishments. Discover how carefully chosen modern artworks can breathe new life into familiar spaces, attracting a younger audience without alienating loyal patrons. Witness the balance between tradition and modernity that revitalizes the overall ambiance.

Consider updating your interiors with carefully curated contemporary art pieces that complement the traditional architecture, creating a dynamic and visually stimulating environment.

Community Engagement: Traditional Businesses in the Digital Age

In "Community Engagement," we explore the role of digital platforms in connecting traditional businesses with a modern audience. Delve into the possibilities of leveraging social media and online galleries to showcase traditional art, tell compelling stories, and engage with a broader community. Witness how a thoughtful online presence can amplify the charm and legacy of traditional establishments.

Consider creating a digital gallery or social media campaign to showcase the artistic aspects of your traditional business, fostering community engagement and attracting a diverse audience.

Conclusion:

In the realm of "Tradition and Modernity: Blending Art Styles in Traditional Businesses," we've unraveled the artful dance between heritage and innovation. From artful entrances and cultural fusion to nostalgic narratives, functional art, modernizing spaces, and community engagement, the possibilities are limitless. As traditional businesses embrace the synergy of tradition and modernity, they create spaces that honor the past while embracing the excitement of the future.

Artful Clicks: Elevating Retail Therapy 2.0 with Creativity in Online Spaces

The Evolution of Retail Therapy

In the age of e-commerce, retail therapy has taken on a new dimension. It's not just about the products; it's about the experience. In this blog post, we'll delve into the realm of Retail Therapy 2.0, exploring the transformative role of art in online spaces. From virtual galleries to interactive websites, discover how the infusion of creativity enhances the online shopping experience and provides a new form of therapy for the modern shopper.

The Digital Gallery - Turning Websites into Virtual Art Spaces

The digital realm offers limitless possibilities, and savvy e-commerce businesses are turning their websites into virtual art galleries. Actively incorporating visually stunning graphics, illustrations, and even animations onto the online platform creates an immersive and aesthetic experience for users. Imagine navigating a website that feels more like strolling through a curated art exhibit than scrolling through product listings.

Active collaboration with digital artists or graphic designers is key to achieving this digital gallery effect. By curating an online space that showcases artistry alongside products, e-commerce businesses not only capture the attention of visitors but also create an emotional connection, turning the act of browsing into a visually delightful and therapeutic experience.

Interactive Aesthetics - Engaging Users Beyond Products

Beyond static images, the future of e-commerce lies in interactive aesthetics. Incorporating elements like 360-degree product views, interactive lookbooks, or augmented reality (AR) features actively engages users beyond the realm of traditional retail. Picture a scenario where customers can virtually try on clothing items or visualize furniture in their own living spaces. This active participation goes beyond the transactional, creating a dynamic and enjoyable shopping journey.

Active collaboration with developers and AR specialists is crucial for implementing interactive features. By embracing interactive aesthetics, e-commerce businesses not only elevate the online shopping experience but also provide a form of retail therapy that goes beyond the tangible, turning the act of browsing and purchasing into a personalized and engaging adventure.

Artful Storytelling - Crafting Narratives Beyond Products

In Retail Therapy 2.0, the narrative goes beyond the products themselves. Artful storytelling through blogs, videos, and even interactive content allows e-commerce businesses to connect with customers on a deeper level. Imagine a clothing brand sharing the journey of their designers, the inspiration behind each collection, or the craftsmanship involved in creating each piece. This active storytelling not only adds layers of meaning to products but also creates a sense of connection and loyalty.

Active collaboration with content creators, writers, and videographers is essential for weaving compelling narratives. By incorporating artful storytelling into their online spaces, e-commerce businesses not only sell products but also sell experiences and emotions. This shift transforms the act of shopping into a therapeutic and immersive journey, making customers feel more connected to the brand.

Personalized Artistry - Tailoring the Shopping Experience

Retail Therapy 2.0 is about personalization, and art plays a significant role in tailoring the shopping experience for individual users. Imagine an online platform that actively suggests products based on a user's preferences, not just in terms of style but also in artistic taste. By analyzing purchase history, browsing behavior, and even demographic data, e-commerce businesses can curate personalized recommendations that align with the unique aesthetics of each user.

Active collaboration with data analysts and AI specialists is crucial for implementing personalized artistry features. By embracing personalized artistry, e-commerce businesses not only enhance the relevance of product recommendations but also create a sense of exclusivity and personal connection, turning the act of shopping into a bespoke and therapeutic experience.

Virtual Storefronts - Creating Immersive Online Environments

In Retail Therapy 2.0, the concept of a storefront transcends physical boundaries. Virtual storefronts and 3D environments allow users to navigate online spaces as if they were exploring a physical store. Picture a virtual boutique where customers can stroll through aisles, interact with products, and even virtually meet other shoppers. This active replication of the in-store experience brings a sense of normalcy and connection to online shopping.

Active collaboration with VR developers and designers is vital for creating immersive virtual storefronts. By incorporating this level of interactivity, e-commerce businesses not only provide a unique and enjoyable shopping experience but also bridge the gap between the online and offline worlds. This artful integration transforms the act of shopping into a form of therapy, where users can escape reality and immerse themselves in a world of curated aesthetics.

Seamless Art Integration - From Browsing to Checkout

In the world of Retail Therapy 2.0, the artful journey doesn't end when a customer decides to make a purchase. Seamless art integration ensures that the aesthetic experience continues seamlessly from browsing to checkout. Visual appeal should extend to every step of the user journey, including product pages, shopping carts, and confirmation screens. Imagine a checkout page that feels like the conclusion of a beautifully crafted story, with art elements that echo the brand's identity and enhance the overall aesthetic.

Active collaboration between UX/UI designers and brand curators is essential for achieving seamless art integration. By ensuring that the artful journey extends to the checkout process, e-commerce businesses not only maintain a consistent aesthetic but also leave a lasting impression on customers. This final touch transforms the act of completing a purchase into a satisfying and visually pleasing conclusion to the retail therapy session.

Beyond Transactions - The Artful Future of E-commerce

In the era of Retail Therapy 2.0, the role of art in e-commerce goes beyond aesthetics; it's about creating meaningful and immersive experiences for the modern shopper. From virtual galleries to interactive aesthetics, personalized artistry, and virtual storefronts, the possibilities are endless. By actively embracing art in online spaces, e-commerce businesses not only draw in customers but also provide a therapeutic journey that transcends the transactional, making the act of shopping a form of artful indulgence.

Interactive Art Installations: Engaging Customers in Unique Ways

Welcome to the world of art that goes beyond mere observation. In "Interactive Art Installations: Engaging Customers in Unique Ways," we'll embark on a journey through the innovative realm where art meets interaction. Get ready to explore how interactive installations are transforming spaces and captivating audiences in unprecedented ways.

Beyond the Frame: Redefining the Art Experience

In "Beyond the Frame," we break free from traditional constraints, exploring how interactive art installations redefine the conventional art experience. Delve into the shift from passive observation to active participation, as visitors become integral parts of the artwork. Discover how artists are challenging the boundaries of artistic expression, creating immersive environments that invite audiences to touch, move, and engage with the art on a personal level.

Consider incorporating interactive installations in gallery spaces, turning the art-viewing experience into a dynamic and participatory adventure.

Digital Dialogues: Navigating the Intersection of Art and Technology

In "Digital Dialogues," we dive into the marriage of art and technology, unveiling the mesmerizing possibilities of digital interactive installations. Explore how advancements in technology enable artists to craft dynamic, responsive, and ever-changing artworks. From interactive projections to augmented reality, witness how artists are leveraging cutting-edge tech to create immersive environments that captivate and challenge the senses.

Consider collaborating with tech-savvy artists to bring digital interactive installations to your space, adding a futuristic flair to the art experience.

Tactile Temptations: The Allure of Touchable Art

In "Tactile Temptations," we explore the irresistible appeal of touchable art installations. Discover how artists are breaking the norm by encouraging visitors to feel, manipulate, and interact physically with the artworks. Dive into the sensory journey where textures, shapes, and materials invite tactile exploration, turning the art-viewing experience into a multi-sensory adventure.

Consider incorporating touchable installations in public spaces, allowing visitors of all ages to experience art through the sense of touch.

Immersive Environments: Stepping Inside the Art

In "Immersive Environments," we step into the heart of art, exploring how interactive installations create immersive worlds that transcend the boundaries between the observer and the observed. Delve into the transformation of spaces into mesmerizing environments, where visitors are no longer spectators but active participants, influencing and becoming a part of the evolving artistic narrative.

Consider designing dedicated spaces for immersive installations, allowing visitors to lose themselves in a world of artistic enchantment.

Audience as Artist: Co-Creation in Interactive Art

In "Audience as Artist," we celebrate the concept of co-creation, where audiences become collaborators in the artistic process. Explore how artists are relinquishing control, allowing visitors to contribute to the evolution of the artwork. Witness the power of collective creativity as interactive installations foster a sense of ownership and connection, blurring the lines between artist and audience.

Consider hosting events that encourage audience participation, turning your space into a dynamic platform for collaborative art creation.

Branding Brilliance: Interactive Installations in Commercial Spaces

In "Branding Brilliance," we uncover the strategic use of interactive art installations in commercial spaces. From retail stores to corporate lobbies, explore how brands are leveraging interactive art to engage customers, enhance brand identity, and create memorable experiences. Witness the fusion of art and commerce, where interactive installations serve as powerful tools for brand storytelling and customer engagement.

Consider incorporating interactive installations in your commercial space, transforming it into a dynamic and memorable brand experience.

Conclusion:

In "Interactive Art Installations: Engaging Customers in Unique Ways," we've navigated through the captivating world where art meets interaction. From redefining the art experience to exploring digital dialogues, tactile temptations, immersive environments, audience co-creation, and branding brilliance, interactive art installations emerge as transformative elements that go beyond aesthetics. Whether you're a gallery owner, event organizer, or brand curator, the integration of interactive art promises to redefine the way audiences engage with and experience art.

Multi-Purpose Spaces: Adaptable Wall Art for Flexible Work Environments

Step into the realm where versatility meets creativity in "Multi-Purpose Spaces: Adaptable Wall Art for Flexible Work Environments." In this journey, we unravel the secrets of transforming dynamic spaces into hubs of inspiration and functionality, using wall art as the key ingredient.

The Essence of Adaptability: Art That Moves with You

In "The Essence of Adaptability," we explore the fundamental concept of flexible work environments. Dive into the art of selecting pieces that seamlessly transition between varied functions of a space. Discover how lightweight, modular, and easily repositionable artworks can be the perfect companions in spaces that wear multiple hats, adapting to the ever-changing needs of the modern workspace.

Consider artworks on movable panels or suspended installations, allowing for effortless reconfiguration of spaces to accommodate different activities.

Transformative Murals: Changing Moods with a Brushstroke

In "Transformative Murals," we embark on a visual journey of how murals can serve as chameleons, changing the ambiance of a space with a single brushstroke. Explore the power of large-scale murals that effortlessly shift the mood from collaborative brainstorming sessions to focused individual work. Dive into the transformative potential of wall art to evoke different emotions and energies, catering to the diverse requirements of a multi-functional environment.

Consider commissioning artists to create murals that capture the essence of each space, enabling a quick shift in atmosphere when needed.

Functional Art: Pieces with Purpose Beyond Aesthetics

In "Functional Art," we delve into the world of wall pieces that transcend mere aesthetics, serving functional purposes within a flexible workspace. From acoustic panels doubling as vibrant canvases to magnetic art that doubles as interactive boards, discover how art can seamlessly integrate with practicality, contributing to the efficiency and adaptability of a multi-purpose space.

Consider incorporating pieces that serve dual purposes, enhancing both the visual appeal and functionality of the workspace.

The Art of Personalization: Tailoring Spaces to Individual Needs

In "The Art of Personalization," we explore how adaptable wall art can contribute to creating personalized workspaces within a larger multifunctional setting. Discover the impact of allowing individuals to customize their immediate surroundings, fostering a sense of ownership and comfort. From personalized prints to adjustable art displays, learn how a touch of personalization can enhance the overall adaptability and satisfaction of employees.

Consider implementing a system that allows employees to rotate or personalize the art in their immediate workspace, promoting a sense of belonging.

Seasonal Splendor: Celebrating Change through Art Installations

In "Seasonal Splendor," we delve into the concept of using art installations to celebrate seasonal changes and holidays. Explore how adaptable wall art can be curated to reflect the spirit of different seasons, bringing a sense of freshness and excitement to the workspace. Dive into the creative possibilities of rotating art displays that align with the rhythm of the calendar, keeping the environment lively and engaging.

Consider creating a calendar of rotating art installations that coincide with different seasons, fostering a dynamic and festive atmosphere.

Tech-Infused Art: Interactive Displays

for Collaborative Spaces

In "Tech-Infused Art," we explore the intersection of technology and wall art in fostering collaboration within flexible work environments. Uncover the potential of interactive displays and digital art installations that promote engagement and teamwork. From digital canvases to interactive projections, discover how technology-integrated art can elevate the functionality of shared spaces, providing tools for effective communication and collaboration.

Consider investing in interactive displays that allow teams to brainstorm, share ideas, and collaborate in real-time, enhancing the adaptability of collaborative spaces.

Conclusion:

In "Multi-Purpose Spaces: Adaptable Wall Art for Flexible Work Environments," we've unveiled the transformative power of art in shaping dynamic and versatile workspaces. From movable artworks to transformative murals, functional art, personalized spaces, seasonal celebrations, and tech-infused displays, wall art emerges as a dynamic force that not only enhances aesthetics but also contributes to the seamless adaptability of modern work environments.

Elevating Expectation: Crafting Artful Waiting Spaces for Clients

The Prelude to Presence

Step into the world of "Elevating Expectation," where the art of waiting transforms reception areas into enchanting spaces for clients. In this blog post, we'll explore the creative alchemy that turns the act of waiting into a memorable and delightful experience. From curated galleries to interactive installations, discover how businesses are setting the stage for positive client interactions.

The Waiting Canvas - Crafting an Artful First Impression

Begin our journey with "Crafting an Artful First Impression," the first chapter that unveils how businesses are using art to make impactful first impressions on clients waiting in reception areas. The waiting room is the initial touchpoint, and businesses are leveraging art to create immersive experiences. Imagine a reception area adorned with dynamic sculptures or an entrance pathway featuring interactive light installations. Crafting an artful first impression not only captivates clients but also sets a positive tone for their overall experience, transforming the act of waiting into an anticipation-filled prelude.

The power of these artistic entrances lies in their ability to create a welcoming and memorable atmosphere. When clients walk into a waiting room and are greeted by thoughtfully curated art, it fosters a sense of excitement and engagement. Businesses recognize that the first impression goes beyond formalities; it's an artful dance that begins with the visual allure of the environment, establishing a foundation for successful client interactions.

Thematic Galleries - Tailoring Art to Industry and Brand Identity

Dive into the second chapter, "Tailoring Art to Industry and Brand Identity," where we explore how businesses are curating thematic galleries that align with their industry and brand identity. Waiting areas are no longer just functional; they are becoming dynamic spaces that reflect the essence of the business. Imagine a law firm with a gallery featuring legal-themed artwork or a tech company with interactive installations showcasing their latest innovations. Thematic galleries not only provide visual interest but also convey a sense of expertise and identity that resonates with clients.

The transformative impact of thematic galleries lies in their ability to create a connection between the art and the business. When clients find themselves surrounded by artwork that mirrors the industry and values of the company, it establishes a subtle but powerful connection. Businesses recognize that these curated spaces go beyond aesthetics; they become visual narratives that convey the essence of the brand, making the waiting experience more immersive and aligned with client expectations.

Interactive Installations - Turning Waiting into Engaging Moments

"Engaging Moments: Interactive Installations" unfolds as the third chapter, showcasing how businesses are turning waiting into dynamic and participatory experiences with interactive installations. Waiting rooms are no longer static spaces; they are evolving into interactive environments that captivate clients. Picture a medical office with touch-sensitive displays providing health tips or a financial institution with interactive projections allowing clients to explore their services. Interactive installations not only engage the senses but also turn waiting into moments of exploration and learning.

The transformative impact of interactive installations lies in their ability to turn the waiting experience into a positive and memorable interaction. When clients can actively participate in creating or interacting with art, it creates shared experiences that enhance their overall perception of the business. Businesses recognize that these interactive exhibits add an element of playfulness to waiting areas, fostering a culture of engagement and transforming idle moments into valuable interactions.

Artful Seating - Sculpting Comfort and Aesthetics

Enter the realm of "Sculpting Comfort and Aesthetics," the fourth chapter that explores how businesses are incorporating artful seating to enhance the waiting experience. Seating is a crucial element of waiting areas, and businesses are turning it into a canvas for both comfort and aesthetics. Imagine a law firm with modern, artistic benches or a design studio with custom-designed seating inspired by their portfolio. Artful seating not only adds a touch of sophistication but also creates a comfortable and visually appealing environment for clients.

The transformative impact of artful seating lies in its ability to sculpt the overall ambiance of the waiting area. When clients find themselves surrounded by seating that is both comfortable and visually aligned with the brand, it enhances their perception of the business. Businesses recognize that the strategic use of art in seating goes beyond functionality; it becomes a means to create an inviting and aesthetically pleasing atmosphere that elevates the waiting experience.

Natural Elements and Biophilic Design - Bringing the Outdoors In

"Bringing the Outdoors In: Natural Elements and Biophilic Design" unfolds as the fifth chapter, showcasing how businesses are incorporating natural elements into waiting areas to create a calming and inviting atmosphere. Waiting rooms are transcending traditional aesthetics and embracing biophilic design, bringing the outdoors inside. Picture a medical clinic with a living wall of plants or a corporate office with natural materials and textures. Biophilic design not only adds a touch of nature but also creates a serene and welcoming environment for clients.

The transformative impact of natural elements and biophilic design lies in their ability to evoke feelings of

tranquility and well-being. When clients are surrounded by the calming presence of nature, it transforms the waiting experience into a moment of relaxation. Businesses recognize that this intentional integration of natural elements not only enhances the aesthetics of the space but also contributes to the overall well-being of clients, making their wait more pleasant and enjoyable.

Curated Experiences - Turning Waiting into a Journey

Conclude our exploration with "Turning Waiting into a Journey," the final chapter that emphasizes the value of curated experiences in waiting areas. Waiting isn't just about passing time; it's an opportunity to create memorable and enjoyable moments. Imagine a hotel with a virtual art tour available on tablets or a car dealership with curated playlists and digital art displays. Curated experiences not only entertain but also turn the waiting journey into an extension of the client's overall interaction with the business.

The beauty of curated experiences lies in their ability to transform waiting into a positive and memorable part of the client's journey. When clients can engage with curated content that aligns with the values and identity of the business, it turns waiting into an intentional and enjoyable experience. Businesses recognize that these curated moments contribute to positive perceptions, making the waiting area an integral part of the overall client experience.

Productivity and Creativity: Enhancing Office Environments with Art

Unleash the transformative power of art in the workplace! In this exploration of "Productivity and Creativity," we embark on a journey to discover how the right artistic choices can supercharge your office environment, fostering an atmosphere that fuels both innovation and efficiency.

The Creative Canvas: Art in Open Workspaces

Step into "The Creative Canvas," where we unravel the impact of art in open workspaces. From dynamic wall murals to strategically placed sculptures, learn how thoughtful art curation in these collaborative areas can inspire creativity, encourage spontaneous idea-sharing, and infuse energy into the daily grind.

Consider rotating art installations periodically to keep the creative canvas ever-evolving, sparking fresh inspiration among employees.

Focus Zones: Sculpting Art for Productivity

In "Focus Zones," we delve into the intricate balance between art and concentration. Discover how curated pieces in designated focus areas can act as visual cues for productivity. Explore the symbiotic relationship between certain art forms and the ability to enhance concentration, helping employees delve into deep, uninterrupted work.

Consider incorporating artwork that resonates with the specific function of each focus zone, creating a tailored and conducive environment.

Colorful Perspectives: The Psychology of Hues in Workspaces

Explore "Colorful Perspectives" and dive into the psychology of hues in workspaces. Uncover the impact of color on mood, focus, and overall well-being. From calming blues to energizing yellows, learn how the strategic use of color through art can create a harmonious environment that supports both productivity and creativity.

Consider conducting a survey among employees to understand color preferences and integrating the most favored tones into your office art palette.

Artful Breaks: Creativity Corners and Relaxation Spaces

In "Artful Breaks," we shift focus to the importance of relaxation areas adorned with carefully chosen art. Discover how thoughtfully curated spaces can provide employees with much-needed breaks, fostering creativity by offering moments of respite. From comfortable seating surrounded by inspiring art to interactive installations, explore ideas to revitalize your break spaces.

Consider creating a rotating gallery of employee-created art to add a personal touch to relaxation spaces, encouraging artistic expression.

Motivation on Display: Art in Employee-centric Areas

In this section, "Motivation on Display," we explore the significance of placing art in areas centered around employees. From hallways to cafeterias, discover how motivational art can contribute to a positive atmosphere, enhancing the overall work experience. Unearth creative ways to align motivational messages with your company's mission and values.

Consider involving employees in the selection process for motivational art, ensuring it resonates with the diverse perspectives within your workforce.

Interactive Installations: Fostering Team Bonding and Innovation

Our final destination, "Interactive Installations," unveils the potential of hands-on art experiences. Learn how installations that invite participation can foster team bonding, innovation, and a shared sense of accomplishment. Delve into the idea that art isn't just for admiration but can serve as a catalyst for collaboration and fresh ideas.

Consider hosting art workshops or team-building activities that involve creating collaborative pieces, enhancing both teamwork and creativity.

Conclusion:

In "Productivity and Creativity: Enhancing Office Environments with Art," we've navigated the multifaceted ways in which art can elevate your workplace. From open spaces to personalized focus zones, each section of this blog post serves as a guide to infusing your office with creativity, productivity, and a renewed sense of purpose.

Art on the Menu: Crafting an Artful Experience in Restaurants and Bars

The Artful Alchemy of Hospitality Design

Step into a world where dining becomes an experience, and the ambiance is as delectable as the menu. In this blog post, we'll explore the delightful synergy of artful design in restaurants and bars, unraveling how carefully curated aesthetics can elevate the dining experience to a visual feast. From avant-garde decor to immersive installations, join us on a journey into the heart of hospitality haven, where every detail is a brushstroke on the canvas of culinary art.

1: The Culinary Canvas - Setting the Tone with Aesthetics

Restaurants and bars are more than places to dine; they're canvases waiting to be adorned with artistic flair. The active infusion of visual elements sets the tone for the entire dining experience. Imagine walking into a restaurant where the decor seamlessly complements the cuisine, creating a cohesive aesthetic journey. From the color palette to the choice of furniture and lighting, every detail contributes to the creation of a welcoming and visually appealing ambiance.

Active collaboration between interior designers and artists is key to achieving an artful balance. By actively curating the culinary canvas, restaurants and bars not only attract patrons but also create a memorable and immersive dining experience. The artful design becomes an integral part of the overall identity, reflecting the essence of the establishment and inviting guests into a world of gastronomic artistry.

2: Ambiance Alchemy - Creating Mood with Artful Lighting

The ambiance of a restaurant or bar is a symphony of elements, and artful lighting plays a starring role. From subtle mood lighting that enhances intimacy to bold installations that make a statement, the active integration of lighting as an art form transforms spaces. Imagine a bar bathed in the warm glow of strategically placed pendant lights, or a restaurant where each table is a spotlight under a constellation of artistic chandeliers.

Active collaboration with lighting designers and artists allows establishments to create bespoke lighting solutions that align with their brand and theme. By actively harnessing the power of ambiance alchemy, restaurants and bars not only elevate the visual appeal of their spaces but also craft an immersive experience where the interplay of light becomes an integral part of the culinary narrative.

3: Artful Fusion - Culinary and Visual Creativity Hand in Hand

In the world of artful design, the fusion of culinary and visual creativity becomes a culinary masterpiece in itself. Imagine dining in a restaurant where the presentation of each dish is a work of art, and the plating is as carefully considered as the decor. Active collaboration between chefs and visual artists can lead to unique and visually stunning presentations that elevate the entire dining experience.

From avant-garde dish presentations to thematic menu designs, the possibilities for artful fusion are boundless. By actively intertwining culinary and visual creativity, restaurants and bars not only tantalize taste buds but also engage diners on a multisensory level. The dining table becomes a canvas, and each course a brushstroke in a gastronomic masterpiece.

4: Immersive Installations - Making Spaces Come Alive

Immersive art installations are the secret sauce for creating a truly unforgettable dining experience. Picture a restaurant adorned with suspended sculptures that dance with the breeze or a bar with interactive digital displays that respond to the patrons' movements. By actively incorporating immersive installations, establishments transform their spaces into living works of art, making every visit a feast for the senses.

Active collaboration with installation artists or digital designers is crucial for creating installations that harmonize with the overall theme of the venue. By actively embracing immersive art, restaurants and bars not only draw in patrons seeking a unique experience but also position themselves as trendsetters in the competitive hospitality landscape.

5: Thematic Threads - Crafting Visual Narratives

Restaurants and bars with a strong visual theme weave a narrative that resonates with diners. The active incorporation of thematic threads, whether inspired by cultural elements, historical periods, or avant-garde concepts, adds depth to the dining experience. Imagine a speakeasy-style bar where every detail, from the decor to the staff uniforms, transports guests to the glamorous era of the Roaring Twenties.

Active collaboration with designers and artists who understand the nuances of thematic design is essential. By actively crafting visual narratives, establishments not only create a memorable dining atmosphere but also immerse guests in a world that goes beyond the plate. The thematic threads become an integral part of the brand identity, fostering a sense of loyalty and connection among patrons.

6: Dynamic Dining - The Ever-Evolving Canvas

In the realm of artful design, restaurants and bars are ever-evolving canvases. The dynamics of hospitality call for constant innovation and adaptation. Actively planning for rotations, seasonal changes, or thematic updates ensures that the visual appeal of the establishment remains fresh and relevant. Imagine a restaurant that transforms its decor to celebrate different cultural festivals or a bar that evolves its theme with the changing seasons.

Active collaboration with interior designers and artists who embrace the concept of dynamic dining is crucial. By actively embracing change and variety, restaurants and bars not only keep patrons coming back for new visual experiences but also position themselves as dynamic and trend-conscious players in the culinary landscape.

Conclusion: Where Art and Flavor Collide

In the world of hospitality, the artful design of restaurants and bars goes beyond mere aesthetics; it's about creating an immersive and unforgettable experience where art and flavor collide. From setting the tone with a carefully curated culinary canvas to crafting dynamic dining spaces that evolve with the seasons, the possibilities are as vast as the culinary creations themselves. Restaurants and bars become havens of artful indulgence, inviting guests to savor not only the flavors on their plates but also the visual feast that surrounds them.

Waltzing Through Walls: The Charismatic Allure of Gallery Walks in Business Spaces

The Dance of Exploration in Business Galleries

Step into the enchanting world of "Waltzing Through Walls," where the magnetic charm of gallery walks transforms ordinary business spaces into dynamic realms of exploration. In this blog post, we'll unravel the magic behind encouraging movement and engagement through curated gallery walks. From corporate lobbies to office hallways, discover how businesses are turning static spaces into vibrant canvases that beckon employees and visitors to waltz through artistic wonders.

1: The Artful Prelude - Setting the Stage for Movement

Begin our journey with "Setting the Stage for Movement," the first chapter that explores how businesses are using art to create an artful prelude, enticing individuals to embark on a journey through the gallery walk. Imagine a corporate entrance adorned with captivating sculptures or a hallway transformed into a visual narrative through carefully curated artworks. Setting the stage for movement not only captures attention but also creates a sense of anticipation, inviting individuals to waltz through the space and explore the visual treasures that lie ahead.

The transformative power of this artful prelude lies in its ability to break the monotony of static business environments. When employees and visitors encounter visually enticing elements at the very entrance, it sparks curiosity and sets a positive tone for their entire experience. Businesses recognize that this strategic use of art serves as a dynamic welcome, encouraging movement and exploration from the moment individuals step through the door.

2: Navigating Narratives - Art as a Guiding Force in Business Spaces

Dive into the second chapter, "Navigating Narratives," where we explore how businesses are turning gallery walks into curated journeys with art serving as a guiding force. The gallery walk isn't just a collection of random artworks; it's a narrative woven through the business space, guiding individuals on a visual expedition. Picture a technology company with a gallery walk showcasing the evolution of their innovations or a healthcare facility with thematic artworks guiding visitors through different medical specialties. Navigating narratives with art not only engages the mind but also transforms the gallery walk into an educational and immersive experience.

The transformative impact of navigating narratives lies in its ability to turn gallery walks into more than just aesthetic encounters. When individuals follow a curated path that tells a story or imparts information, it transforms the act of walking through the gallery into a purposeful and enriching journey. Businesses recognize that this intentional curation not only enhances the overall experience but also ensures that movement through the space is purposeful and meaningful.

3: Thematic Enclaves - Creating Dynamic Spaces within Business Walls

"Creating Dynamic Spaces within Business Walls" unfolds as the third chapter, showcasing how businesses are carving out thematic enclaves within the gallery walk to elevate the experience. The gallery walk isn't a uniform stretch of artworks; it's a collection of dynamic spaces, each with its own theme and personality. Imagine an advertising agency with a section dedicated to visualizing brand campaigns or a financial institution with a themed enclave highlighting the history of finance. Thematic enclaves not only add variety but also create memorable pockets of exploration within the gallery walk, encouraging individuals to pause and absorb the nuances of each theme.

The transformative impact of thematic enclaves lies in their ability to cater to diverse interests and preferences. When individuals encounter pockets of themed artworks, it allows for deeper engagement, as they can choose to linger in areas that resonate with their personal or professional interests. Businesses recognize that these thematic spaces contribute to a more dynamic and personalized gallery walk experience, ensuring that movement is not just about traversing distance but also about immersing oneself in curated content.

4: Interactive Stations - Turning Movement into Engagement Opportunities

Enter the realm of "Turning Movement into Engagement Opportunities," the fourth chapter that explores how businesses are incorporating interactive stations within the gallery walk to transform passive movement into active engagement. The gallery walk isn't a one-way street; it's a dynamic avenue where individuals can actively participate in the experience. Picture a tech company with touch-sensitive displays providing insights into their latest projects or a creative agency with interactive art installations that invite individuals to contribute their own artistic expressions. Interactive stations not only break the barrier between observer and artwork but also turn movement through the gallery into moments of hands-on exploration.

The transformative impact of interactive stations lies in their ability to turn the gallery walk into a dynamic and participatory journey. When individuals can actively engage with art, whether through touch, interaction, or contribution, it elevates the entire experience. Businesses recognize that these interactive elements not only add layers of interest but also contribute to a culture of active exploration and creativity within the business space.

5: Rotating Exhibits - Infusing Freshness into Familiar Paths

"Infusing Freshness into Familiar Paths" unfolds as the fifth chapter, showcasing how businesses are keeping gallery walks dynamic by introducing rotating exhibits. The gallery walk doesn't remain static; it evolves over time with the infusion of new artworks and themes. Imagine a corporate office with quarterly rotations introducing fresh perspectives from local artists or a business hub that collaborates with employees for periodic exhibits showcasing their talents. Rotating exhibits not only prevent gallery

walks from becoming mundane but also create a sense of anticipation, encouraging individuals to revisit familiar paths with the excitement of discovering something new.

The transformative power of rotating exhibits lies in their

ability to keep the gallery walk dynamic and ever-evolving. When individuals know that the artworks along their usual paths might change, it adds an element of surprise and curiosity to their daily movements within the business space. Businesses recognize that this infusion of freshness ensures that the gallery walk remains a vibrant and ever-changing canvas, enticing individuals to keep waltzing through familiar yet perpetually exciting paths.

6: Employee Involvement - A Collaborative Dance Through Business Galleries

Conclude our exploration with "A Collaborative Dance Through Business Galleries," the final chapter that emphasizes the role of employee involvement in shaping the gallery walk experience. The gallery walk isn't solely curated by management; it's a collaborative dance where employees contribute to the vibrancy of the space. Imagine a company fostering an art program where employees can submit their artworks for display or a collaborative mural project in a communal area. Employee involvement not only adds a personal touch but also turns the gallery walk into a collective expression of the diverse talents within the business.

The transformative impact of employee involvement lies in its ability to turn the gallery walk into a shared experience. When employees actively contribute to the artworks or themes, it creates a sense of ownership and pride in the gallery walk. Businesses recognize that this collaborative dance not only fosters a positive and creative workplace culture but also ensures that the gallery walk is a reflection of the collective spirit within the organization.

Beyond Shelves: The Artful Symphony of Merchandising Magic with Wall Art in Retail Spaces

The Canvas of Retail Innovation

Step into the world of retail innovation where products are not just displayed but curated as part of an artful symphony. In this blog post, we explore the dynamic realm of artful merchandising, where wall art becomes a powerful tool for highlighting products in retail spaces. From strategic displays to immersive installations, discover how the fusion of art and retail is reshaping the way businesses showcase their offerings.

The Power of Visual Narratives - Transforming Walls into Storytelling Canvases

Unlock the first chapter, "The Power of Visual Narratives," where walls cease to be mere partitions and transform into storytelling canvases. Artful merchandising begins with the strategic use of wall art to tell a compelling narrative about the products on display. Consider murals that illustrate the journey of a product from creation to consumer, or thematic installations that evoke the essence of a brand. By weaving visual stories through wall art, businesses create immersive environments that captivate customers and guide them through a curated experience.

The power of visual narratives goes beyond aesthetics; it shapes the perception and emotional connection customers have with the products. As customers move through a space adorned with carefully chosen wall art, they become part of a visual journey that enhances their overall shopping experience. In this way, walls become dynamic storytellers, communicating not just the features but the essence of the products on display.

Strategic Product Displays - Merging Form and Function

Dive into "Strategic Product Displays," the second chapter that delves into the marriage of form and function. Artful merchandising involves not just what is on the shelves but how products are visually presented. Businesses are strategically using wall art to complement and enhance product displays. Imagine a boutique with wall-mounted art frames that perfectly align with the aesthetics of adjacent clothing racks or a tech store with digital displays seamlessly integrated into a mural showcasing the latest gadgets. These strategic displays not only grab attention but also create a cohesive and visually pleasing shopping environment.

The key here is to merge form and function seamlessly. Wall art should not overshadow the products but enhance their appeal. By strategically placing art in proximity to products, businesses create a visual harmony that elevates the perceived value of the items on display. In this way, every inch of the retail space becomes an opportunity to showcase products in a manner that is both functional and aesthetically pleasing.

Themed Environments - Elevating Shopping to an Experience

"Themed Environments" emerge as the third chapter, unveiling how businesses are elevating shopping from a transaction to an experience. Artful merchandising extends beyond individual product displays to the creation of themed environments that immerse customers in a curated world. Imagine a bookstore with literary-inspired murals, or a sports gear store with a dynamic wall installation capturing the energy of various sports. Themed environments transform retail spaces into destinations, inviting customers to explore and connect with products in a context that resonates with their interests and aspirations.

The beauty of themed environments lies in their ability to evoke emotions and create memorable experiences. When customers step into a space that aligns with a particular theme, they feel a sense of belonging and connection. By using wall art to craft these thematic experiences, businesses not only highlight products but also invite customers into a world where shopping becomes an immersive and enjoyable adventure.

Interactive Displays - Engaging Customers Beyond the Shelves

Enter the realm of "Interactive Displays," the fourth chapter that explores how businesses are engaging customers beyond the traditional shelves. Artful merchandising embraces technology and interactivity to transform walls into dynamic displays. Picture a cosmetic store with a digital mirror that allows customers to virtually try on different makeup looks, or a furniture store with touch-sensitive screens embedded in a mural, enabling customers to customize and visualize products. Interactive displays go beyond showcasing products; they invite customers to actively participate in the shopping process.

The interactive element adds a layer of engagement and personalization to the retail experience. When customers can touch, explore, and interact with products through wall displays, it creates a memorable and participatory journey. Businesses leverage technology and art to break down the barriers between the physical and digital realms, turning walls into gateways for customers to explore products in innovative and interactive ways.

Seasonal Transformations - Adapting Spaces to Capture the Zeitgeist

"Seasonal Transformations" unfold as the fifth chapter, showcasing how businesses adapt spaces to capture the zeitgeist of different seasons and occasions. Artful merchandising embraces the flexibility of wall art to transform retail spaces according to seasonal themes, holidays, or special events. Imagine a clothing store with ever-changing wall murals that reflect the colors and moods of each season, or a home decor shop with thematic installations that evolve with major holidays. Seasonal transformations create a sense of dynamism and freshness, enticing customers to return and discover what's new.

The ability to adapt spaces to capture the essence of different seasons ensures that retail environments stay relevant and engaging. It allows businesses to align with the cultural and emotional currents of specific times, creating a connection with customers who appreciate the thoughtfulness and relevance of the displays. Seasonal transformations, facilitated by artful merchandising, turn retail spaces into ever-evolving showcases that celebrate the spirit of the moment.

Community Collaborations - Showcasing Local Talent and Building Connections

Conclude our exploration with "
Community Collaborations," the final chapter that emphasizes how businesses are showcasing local talent and building connections through artful merchandising. Wall art becomes a platform for collaboration with local artists, photographers, or artisans, infusing retail spaces with a unique and community-driven character. Picture a grocery store with rotating displays featuring local artists' interpretations of fresh produce, or a fashion boutique that regularly features limited-edition collections crafted by local designers. Community collaborations not only highlight products but also strengthen the ties between businesses and the local creative ecosystem.

The beauty of community collaborations lies in their ability to make retail spaces more than just places to buy products; they become hubs of local culture and expression. By featuring the work of local artists, businesses actively contribute to the cultural richness of their communities and build meaningful connections with residents. Community collaborations, woven into the fabric of artful merchandising, turn retail spaces into dynamic expressions of local identity and creativity.

Retail Storytelling: Using Wall Art to Convey Brand Narratives

Step into the world where art meets commerce, and discover the magic of "Retail Storytelling: Using Wall Art to Convey Brand Narratives." In this exploration, we'll unravel the potent connection between visual storytelling and retail spaces, understanding how curated wall art can transform a store into a narrative-driven experience that resonates with customers.

1. *The Art of First Impressions: Welcoming Shoppers with Impact*

In "The Art of First Impressions," we delve into the importance of creating a captivating entrance that sets the stage for the retail narrative. Explore how strategically placed wall art can grab attention, evoke emotions, and provide an immediate sense of what the brand stands for. Witness the transformative power of impactful visuals in making a lasting impression on shoppers, inviting them to step into a world carefully crafted by design.

Consider integrating brand-focused artwork at the entrance, ensuring that it aligns with your brand's ethos and captivates the attention of passersby.

2. *Thematic Galleries: Curating Stories Within Store Sections*

In "Thematic Galleries," we explore the concept of creating mini art galleries within specific sections of a retail space.

Discover how brands can tell different aspects of their story through curated art that complements the products on display. Explore the idea of thematic storytelling, where each section unfolds a unique chapter, creating a seamless and immersive journey for shoppers.

Consider designing thematic galleries for various product categories, enhancing the overall shopping experience and encouraging customers to explore the entire store.

3. Brand Chronicles: Historical Narratives Through Visual Displays

In "Brand Chronicles," we uncover the fascinating world of historical storytelling within retail spaces. Explore how brands can narrate their evolution, milestones, and values through carefully curated displays. Witness the integration of historical artifacts, archival images, and artistic representations that not only educate customers about the brand's journey but also create a sense of connection and loyalty.

Consider incorporating a "brand chronicle" wall within your store, allowing customers to engage with the evolution and rich history of your brand.

4. Interactive Narratives: Engaging Customers in the Storytelling

In "Interactive Narratives," we explore the dynamic intersection of technology and art, where interactive displays contribute to the retail storytelling experience. Learn how brands use augmented reality, QR codes, or touch-sensitive displays to provide customers with deeper insights into product stories, ethical practices, and the overall brand narrative. Witness how interactivity enhances customer engagement, making shopping not just a transaction but an immersive journey.

Consider integrating interactive displays that allow customers to delve deeper into product details, stories, or behind-the-scenes content.

5. Seasonal Sagas: Evolving Narratives with Timely Themes

In "Seasonal Sagas," we explore the art of adapting retail narratives to reflect seasonal changes, festivities, or cultural events. Witness how brands transform their spaces with seasonal wall art that not only aligns with the current ambiance but also keeps the retail environment fresh and dynamic. Explore the impact of timely and relevant narratives in creating a sense of anticipation and excitement among customers.

Consider planning seasonal updates to your wall art, ensuring that your store remains visually appealing and aligned with ongoing themes and trends.

6. Empowering Customers as Co-Authors: User-Generated Content Walls

In "Empowering Customers as Co-Authors," we discover the rising trend of user-generated content walls, where brands invite customers to contribute to the storytelling. Explore how social media integration, contests, or dedicated spaces for customer artwork create a collaborative narrative, turning customers into co-authors of the brand's story. Witness the power of community engagement in fostering a sense of belonging and brand advocacy.

Consider dedicating a section of your store to showcase customer-generated content, turning your customers into active participants in your brand's storytelling.

To Sum Up:

In "Retail Storytelling: Using Wall Art to Convey Brand Narratives," we've journeyed through the artful fusion of commerce and storytelling, understanding how curated wall art can transform retail spaces into immersive brand experiences. From creating impactful entrances to thematic galleries, brand chronicles, interactive narratives, seasonal sagas, and empowering customers as co-authors, the possibilities are endless. As you embark on curating your retail narrative through wall art, remember that each piece contributes to a larger story that resonates with your customers, fostering a deeper connection and loyalty to your brand.

Artful Affair: Crafting Event Identity Beyond Logos

The Symphony of Art and Event Identity

Embark on a journey into the world of "Artful Affair," where the marriage of art and event identity goes beyond logos. In this blog post, we explore the pivotal role that art plays in shaping the unique character and identity of events. From immersive installations to thematic experiences, discover how businesses are using art as a powerful tool to elevate event branding.

1: The Canvas Unveiled - Art as the Heartbeat of Event Identity

Begin our exploration with "Art as the Heartbeat of Event Identity," the first chapter that delves into how businesses are using art to breathe life into the core of event identity. While logos serve as visual signatures, art becomes the soul that encapsulates the essence and theme of an event. Imagine a product launch with an immersive art installation reflecting the brand's innovation or a gala dinner with thematic artworks that set the mood. Art as the heartbeat of event identity not only engages attendees visually but also becomes a memorable and emotive touchpoint, making the event distinct and resonant.

The transformative power of infusing art into event identity lies in its ability to convey a story beyond words. When attendees step into an environment where art is seamlessly integrated, it becomes a dynamic and immersive experience. Businesses recognize that the canvas of an event, unveiled through carefully chosen art, not only sparks curiosity but also creates a lasting impression that extends far beyond the event itself.

2: Thematic Art Installations - Weaving Narratives That Resonate

Dive into the second chapter, "Weaving Narratives That Resonate," where we explore how businesses are using thematic art installations to create cohesive and compelling event narratives. Thematic installations go beyond mere decoration; they become integral elements that thread a narrative throughout the event. Picture a technology conference with interactive installations showcasing the evolution of the industry or a cultural festival adorned with art that celebrates diversity and inclusion. Thematic art installations not only engage attendees on a deeper level but also contribute to the overall storytelling, making the event more immersive and memorable.

The transformative impact of thematic art installations lies in their ability to shape the narrative and atmosphere of the event. When attendees encounter art that aligns with the event theme, it becomes a visual language that communicates the purpose and values of the gathering. Businesses recognize that these installations serve as powerful storytellers, turning events into multi-sensory experiences that leave a lasting imprint on attendees.

3: Interactive Art Experiences - Engaging Attendees in the Creation of Memories

"Engaging Attendees in the Creation of Memories" unfolds as the third chapter, showcasing how businesses are incorporating interactive art experiences to foster engagement and leave a lasting impression. Attendees are no longer passive observers; they become active participants in the creation of event memories. Imagine a corporate retreat with collaborative mural painting or a product launch with digital art installations that respond to attendee interactions. Interactive art experiences not only break down barriers between the event and the audience but also create a sense of ownership and connection that extends beyond the event timeframe.

The transformative power of interactive art experiences lies in their ability to turn attendees into co-creators of the event identity. When individuals engage with art in a hands-on or digital manner, it transforms the event from a fleeting experience into a participatory journey. Businesses recognize that these interactive moments contribute to a sense of community, making the event identity not just about what happens but also about the shared memories created together.

4: Ambient Art as Event Atmosphere - Setting the Mood Beyond Decor

Enter the realm of "Setting the Mood Beyond Decor," the fourth chapter that explores how ambient art becomes a key player in shaping the overall atmosphere of an event. Beyond serving as decorative elements, ambient art pieces contribute to the mood, energy, and ambiance of the gathering. Picture a fashion show with dynamic light installations that evolve with the music or a gala dinner with ethereal sculptures creating an immersive dining experience. Ambient art as event atmosphere not only adds visual interest but also becomes a dynamic force that influences the emotional tone of the event.

The transformative impact of ambient art lies in its ability to transcend traditional event decor. When businesses strategically use ambient art to create specific atmospheres, it becomes a non-verbal communicator that influences the emotions of attendees. Businesses recognize that the careful selection of ambient art can elevate the event identity, making it a sensorial journey that leaves a lasting imprint on the hearts and minds of those in attendance.

5: Artful Branding Elements - Infusing Corporate Identity into Events

"Dazzling Branding Elements" unfolds as the fifth chapter, showcasing how businesses are infusing their corporate identity into events through artful branding elements. Beyond logos and banners, branding becomes a seamless and integral part of the artistic landscape. Imagine a product launch with branded sculptures that reflect the company's ethos or a corporate conference with custom-designed artworks that embody the organization's values. Artful branding elements not only reinforce corporate identity but also become memorable focal points that anchor the event in the minds of attendees.

The transformative power of artful branding elements lies in their ability to reinforce brand recognition and strengthen the connection between the company and its audience. When attendees encounter branding seamlessly integrated into the artistic elements of the event, it creates a cohesive and unified experience. Businesses recognize that these artful branding elements serve as visual ambassadors, ensuring that the event identity aligns seamlessly with the broader narrative of the organization.

6: Event Identity as an Artful Legacy
- Beyond the Event Horizon

Conclude our exploration with "Beyond the Event Horizon," the final chapter that emphasizes how businesses are creating artful legacies with lasting impacts. Event identity is not confined to the duration of the gathering; it extends beyond the event horizon

, leaving a lasting impression on attendees. Imagine a conference with an art exhibit that tours globally or a product launch with limited edition prints that become sought-after collector's items. Event identity as an artful legacy not only immortalizes the experience but also becomes a powerful tool for post-event engagement and brand recall.

The beauty of event identity as an artful legacy lies in its ability to transcend the temporal boundaries of the event. When businesses strategically leverage art to create tangible artifacts or experiences that outlast the event itself, it becomes a powerful storytelling tool. Businesses recognize that these artful legacies contribute to the long-term resonance of the event, ensuring that the impact and memories endure in the hearts and minds of attendees.

Employee Engagement: Encouraging Ownership of Office Art Choices

Welcome to a workplace where creativity meets ownership in "Employee Engagement: Encouraging Ownership of Office Art Choices." In this blog post, we'll explore the profound impact of involving employees in the art selection process, fostering a sense of belonging, and transforming the office into a canvas where each stroke of creativity is a shared masterpiece.

The Power of Choice: Empowering Employees Through Art

In "The Power of Choice," we unravel the significance of giving employees a say in the selection of office art. Dive into how the freedom to choose artworks cultivates a sense of empowerment, allowing individuals to shape their immediate work environment. Discover the positive effects on morale and motivation when employees feel a personal connection to the art that surrounds them, creating a workplace that reflects their unique tastes and preferences.

Consider implementing a system that allows employees to vote or propose artworks, turning the office into a collaborative art gallery.

Curating Collaboratively: Fostering Team-Building Through Art

In "Curating Collaboratively," we explore the team-building potential of involving employees in the curation of office art.

Dive into the dynamics of collaborative art selection sessions, where teams collectively choose pieces that resonate with their shared values and goals. Discover how this collaborative effort not only enhances team cohesion but also results in a diverse and vibrant office art collection that mirrors the collective spirit of the workforce.

Consider organizing team-building activities around art curation sessions, turning the selection process into a shared experience.

Beyond Aesthetics: Art as a Reflection of Company Culture

In "Beyond Aesthetics," we delve into the idea of using office art as a reflection of company culture. Explore how involving employees in the selection process ensures that the chosen artworks align with the company's values and ethos. Discover the potential of creating a visual narrative within the office space that tells the story of the organization, fostering a strong sense of identity and connection among employees.

Consider conducting surveys or workshops to understand employees' perceptions of the company culture and using that insight to guide art choices.

Art as Conversation Starters: Breaking Down Communication Barriers

In "Art as Conversation Starters," we unravel the communicative power of office art in encouraging dialogue among employees. Explore how strategically chosen artworks serve as conversation starters, promoting interaction and breaking down communication barriers. Discover the impact of shared visual interests in sparking conversations that go beyond work tasks, contributing to a more open and connected workplace.

Consider placing art in communal spaces where employees naturally gather, fostering organic discussions and connections.

Employee Showcases: Highlighting Individual Talent and Perspectives

In "Employee Showcases," we celebrate the individual talents and perspectives of employees by featuring their artworks within the office. Dive into the transformative effect of turning the workplace into a gallery that showcases the diverse talents of the workforce. Discover how such showcases not only recognize and appreciate individual creativity but also inspire a culture of continuous learning and artistic expression.

Consider organizing regular art exhibitions or rotating displays featuring artworks created by employees, turning the office into a dynamic gallery space.

Sustainability and Wellbeing: The Holistic Impact of Employee-Influenced Art

In "Sustainability and Wellbeing," we explore the holistic impact of employee-influenced office art on sustainability and wellbeing. Dive into the potential of creating a healthier and more environmentally conscious workplace by choosing sustainable and locally sourced artworks. Discover how the integration of nature-inspired and wellness-focused art contributes to a more positive and balanced work environment.

Consider adopting eco-friendly art choices and incorporating nature-inspired elements to enhance the overall wellbeing of employees.

Conclusion:

In "Employee Engagement: Encouraging Ownership of Office Art Choices," we've navigated the transformative journey of involving employees in the art selection process. From empowering individuals through choice to fostering team-building, reflecting company culture, breaking down communication barriers, showcasing employee talents, and promoting sustainability and wellbeing, employee engagement in office art choices emerges as a powerful catalyst for a vibrant, connected, and inspired workplace.

Brushing Diversity: A Palette of Inclusive Art Choices

Embracing Colors of Diversity

Art has the incredible power to transcend boundaries and connect people from different walks of life. In a world that thrives on diversity, it's essential to create spaces that reflect the richness of varied cultures, perspectives, and identities. In this blog post, we will explore the concept of inclusive art choices and how they contribute to the celebration of diversity in our surroundings.

The Power of Inclusive Art

Art is a universal language that speaks to the soul, and when curated thoughtfully, it becomes a powerful tool for fostering inclusivity. Inclusive art choices encompass a wide range of mediums, styles, and cultural influences, creating a tapestry that mirrors the mosaic of the human experience. Whether it's paintings, sculptures, or multimedia installations, the goal is to represent the multitude of voices that exist in our global community.

Active voice and dynamic brushstrokes guide the viewer through a journey of cultural appreciation, breaking down barriers and building bridges of understanding. These artworks become catalysts for dialogue, sparking conversations about the beauty found in our differences. By actively choosing art that celebrates diversity, we contribute to the creation of welcoming environments that encourage mutual respect and understanding.

Breaking Stereotypes Through Art

Art has the transformative ability to challenge preconceived notions and break down stereotypes that persist in our society. Inclusive art choices defy expectations and showcase the depth and complexity of various cultures. When curating spaces, consider selecting pieces that challenge traditional narratives, offering alternative perspectives that broaden minds and foster a more inclusive mindset.

By actively seeking out art that challenges stereotypes, we create environments that invite individuals to question assumptions and engage in meaningful conversations. This shift in perspective not only promotes diversity but also contributes to the dismantling of harmful biases, fostering a more inclusive and understanding community.

Showcasing Underrepresented Voices

In the vast world of art, certain voices have historically been marginalized or silenced. Inclusive art choices involve intentional efforts to amplify these voices, ensuring that underrepresented artists have a platform to express their unique experiences and perspectives. Galleries, museums, and public spaces can become advocates for diversity by showcasing the works of artists from marginalized communities.

Active promotion of diversity in art not only empowers individual artists but also sends a powerful message about the value of every narrative. By giving visibility to underrepresented voices, we contribute to a more inclusive cultural landscape that celebrates the richness of human experience in all its forms.

Cultural Fusion in Artistic Expression

Art has the magical ability to merge various cultural elements into a harmonious symphony of creativity. Inclusive art choices embrace cultural fusion, inviting artists to draw inspiration from diverse traditions, aesthetics, and symbolism. The result is a vibrant tapestry that reflects the interconnectedness of our global society.

Actively seeking out and appreciating culturally diverse artworks opens the door to cross-cultural understanding. It encourages viewers to appreciate the beauty found in the amalgamation of different cultural influences, fostering a sense of unity in diversity. By celebrating cultural fusion in art, we contribute to a world where various traditions coexist and thrive, creating a richer and more interconnected global community.

Art as a Tool for Social Change

Art has the power to inspire social change by addressing pressing issues and advocating for justice. Inclusive art choices often involve selecting pieces that shed light on social inequalities, discrimination, and human rights issues. By actively engaging with art that speaks to these topics, individuals and communities can become catalysts for positive change.

Artistic expression has historically played a pivotal role in shaping societal attitudes and influencing change. Through inclusive art choices, we contribute to a collective effort to address systemic issues and foster a more equitable and just world. Art becomes a dynamic force that mobilizes communities, encourages activism, and amplifies the voices of those who are often marginalized.

Curating Inclusive Spaces for the Future

In our ever-evolving world, the responsibility to create inclusive spaces lies in the hands of curators, designers, and art enthusiasts alike. Embracing diversity through art choices is an ongoing journey that requires intentionality and a commitment to continuous learning. As we look to the future, let's envision a world where every art space reflects the kaleidoscope of human experience, fostering understanding, appreciation, and unity.

By actively seeking out and celebrating diverse artworks, we contribute to the creation of inclusive spaces that transcend boundaries and connect us all. Let us be the curators of a future where art is a beacon of diversity, guiding us toward a world where every voice is heard, and every story is valued.

The Art of Inclusivity

In the grand canvas of life, diversity is the vibrant palette that adds depth, beauty, and meaning. Through inclusive art choices, we paint a picture of a world where everyone's story is acknowledged and celebrated. Let us continue to embrace the power of art to foster inclusivity, challenge stereotypes, amplify underrepresented voices, celebrate cultural fusion, and drive positive social change. In doing so, we actively contribute to a future where the world is not just seen but experienced in all its diverse and glorious hues.

Brush of the Moment: The Art of Ephemeral Installations for Business Events

The Magic of Fleeting Beauty

In the fast-paced world of business events, where impressions matter, the ephemeral beauty of temporary art installations is capturing the spotlight. This blog post is your guide to the enchanting realm of ephemeral art, exploring how these fleeting creations can transform your business events, leaving lasting memories and creating an atmosphere that is as dynamic as it is captivating.

The Brief Brilliance - Unveiling the Concept of Ephemeral Art

Ephemeral art, by definition, is transient and impermanent. It's the art of the moment, designed to exist briefly but impact profoundly. In the context of business events, ephemeral installations offer a unique way to engage attendees and create a sense of exclusivity. Whether it's live painting performances, temporary sculptures, or interactive installations, these creations become a living part of the event, sparking conversations and forging memorable connections.

The brief brilliance of ephemeral art lies in its ability to infuse energy and excitement into an event. Attendees are not merely spectators; they are participants in a momentary artistic experience. The impermanence adds an element of urgency, encouraging people to fully immerse themselves in the present, knowing that the art they are witnessing is a once-in-a-lifetime spectacle.

Evolving Spaces - Transformative Impact on Event Venues

Ephemeral installations have the power to redefine event spaces, turning mundane venues into immersive experiences. Whether it's transforming a blank wall into a vibrant mural or temporarily converting an empty corner into a pop-up art studio, these installations breathe life into the surroundings. Attendees find themselves in an ever-evolving environment, creating a sense of anticipation and wonder as they explore the dynamic art landscape.

Consider collaborating with local artists or art collectives to curate installations that resonate with the theme of your event. This not only supports the local arts community but also adds a layer of authenticity to the temporary transformation. The evolving spaces become conversation starters, ensuring that your event is remembered not just for its content but for the artistic journey attendees embarked upon.

Interactive Alchemy - Engaging Attendees Through Participation

Ephemeral art isn't just to be observed; it's meant to be experienced. Incorporating interactive elements into temporary installations adds an extra dimension to your business events. From collaborative murals that attendees contribute to throughout the event to live art performances where participants become part of the creative process, interactive alchemy transforms your event into a dynamic and engaging affair.

Encourage attendees to embrace their creativity by providing interactive stations or workshops. These could include areas for quick sketches, paint-and-sip sessions, or even collaborative digital art projects. The result is not only a physical representation of the event but a collective masterpiece co-created by everyone present, fostering a sense of community and shared experience.

The Art of Brand Storytelling - Crafting Narratives Through Temporal Beauty

Ephemeral art offers a unique canvas for brand storytelling. By aligning installations with your brand narrative, you create a visual and emotional connection with attendees. Consider incorporating elements of your brand identity into temporary sculptures or using the art to convey a specific message or campaign theme. This not only reinforces brand recall but also allows your business event to become a storytelling platform that engages and resonates with your audience.

For example, if launching a new product, consider an ephemeral installation that symbolizes the essence of the product or its journey. If celebrating a milestone, curate art that reflects the evolution and growth of your brand. The art becomes a living testament to your brand story, etching it into the memories of everyone present at the event.

The Spectacle of Unveiling - Creating Memorable Event Moments

Ephemeral installations lend themselves perfectly to grand

unveilings, creating memorable moments that linger in the minds of attendees. Imagine the anticipation as a curtain drops, revealing a stunning mural created right before their eyes or the awe-inspiring moment when a temporary light installation bathes the venue in a spectrum of colors. These spectacles become the highlights of your event, generating buzz and social media traction.

Consider coordinating the timing of installations with key moments in your event schedule, such as product launches, keynote speeches, or award ceremonies. The element of surprise and the visual impact of the unveiling transform these moments into unforgettable experiences, elevating the overall perception of your business event.

Leaving a Lasting Impression - Ephemeral Art Beyond the Event

While ephemeral art is designed to be temporary, its impact can endure far beyond the event itself. Capture the essence of the installations through professional photography and videography. Share these visuals on your company's social media channels, creating a digital footprint that extends the life of the ephemeral art. Consider creating limited-edition prints or digital downloads of the installations as event mementos for attendees.

Additionally, leverage the ephemeral art experience to foster ongoing engagement with your audience. Encourage attendees to share their own photos and reflections on the art on social media platforms, creating a post-event conversation. By extending the life of ephemeral art through digital channels, you ensure that the magic lives on, leaving a lasting impression on both attendees and those who missed the event.

A Symphony of Fleeting Beauty - Mastering Ephemeral Art for Business Events

In the canvas of business events, ephemeral art is the symphony of fleeting beauty, creating moments that resonate and linger. By embracing the impermanence, you unlock a realm of creativity and engagement that goes beyond traditional event experiences. Whether it's transforming spaces, engaging attendees, or crafting narratives, ephemeral art adds a magical touch to your business events, ensuring that each gathering becomes a masterpiece in the art of the moment.

Whimsy at Work: The Playful Symphony of Artful Fun in Office Spaces

Setting the Stage for Workplace Whimsy

Step into the world of Workplace Whimsy, where the ordinary transforms into the extraordinary through the enchanting power of art. In this blog post, we explore how businesses are injecting fun into office spaces with the strategic use of playful art. From whimsical installations to interactive murals, discover the creative inspirations that are reshaping the dynamics of work environments and fostering a culture of joy, collaboration, and innovation.

The Joyful Gateway - Enchanting Entrances to Uplift Spirits

Embark on our journey with "Enchanting Entrances to Uplift Spirits," the first chapter that unveils how businesses are using art to create joyful gateways into the workday. The entrance to an office sets the tone for the entire day, and businesses are leveraging art to infuse positivity from the moment employees step through the door. Imagine a reception area adorned with a vibrant, larger-than-life sculpture that welcomes everyone with a sense of playfulness or a doorway transformed into a whimsical portal through the use of colorful and dynamic installations. Enchanting entrances become the playful preamble to the workday, uplifting spirits and inviting employees into a space that radiates joy and creativity.

The impact of enchanting entrances extends beyond aesthetics; it sets a positive and energizing atmosphere. When employees enter a workplace that embraces whimsical art, it fosters a sense of excitement and anticipation. As businesses recognize the potential of joyful gateways, they actively contribute to a workplace culture that values happiness and creativity.

Artful Workstations - Transforming Desks into Creative Playgrounds

Dive into the second chapter, "Transforming Desks into Creative Playgrounds," where we explore how businesses are redefining workstations with artful playfulness. Workspaces are no longer confined to sterile cubicles; they are evolving into dynamic environments where desks become canvases for creative expression. Imagine an office where each desk features a personalized mural or a team area adorned with interactive elements that encourage spontaneous moments of play. Artful workstations not only break the monotony of traditional office setups but also foster a sense of individuality and ownership among employees.

The transformative impact of artful workstations lies in their ability to enhance the overall work experience. When employees are surrounded by playful art at their desks, it creates a vibrant and stimulating environment that fuels creativity and productivity. Businesses are recognizing that the integration of art into workstations is a powerful tool for fostering a sense of identity and infusing a playful spirit into everyday tasks.

Whimsical Breakout Spaces - Nurturing Creativity and Collaboration

"Creative Corners and Collaborative Corners" unfolds as the third chapter, showcasing how businesses are transforming break areas into whimsical havens that nurture creativity and collaboration. Breakout spaces are no longer just functional; they are becoming vibrant hubs where employees can recharge and connect. Imagine a breakroom with walls adorned with interactive murals that encourage impromptu brainstorming sessions or a lounge area with playful sculptures that serve as focal points for casual discussions. Whimsical breakout spaces create environments that inspire innovation and foster spontaneous interactions among team members.

The transformative impact of these creative corners lies in their ability to break down barriers and encourage socialization. When employees have access to whimsical breakout spaces, it creates a sense of community and belonging. Businesses are recognizing that these areas play a crucial role in cultivating a culture of creativity and collaboration, where the lines between work and play seamlessly blur.

Interactive Installations - Engaging Minds and Encouraging Play

Enter the realm of "Interactive Installations," the fourth chapter that explores how businesses are engaging minds and encouraging play with dynamic and participatory art. Art is no longer a passive element; it's becoming an active player in the workplace experience. Picture an office with interactive installations that respond to touch, sound, or movement, turning hallways into immersive experiences or collaborative spaces with digital displays that invite employees to contribute their ideas in real-time. Interactive installations go beyond decoration; they become catalysts for play, encouraging employees to explore and interact with their surroundings.

The transformative impact of interactive installations lies in their ability to engage employees on multiple levels. When art becomes a medium for interaction, it creates a dynamic and participatory workplace culture. Businesses are recognizing that the integration of interactive installations not only adds an element of playfulness to the office but also stimulates creativity and innovation by providing employees with unconventional outlets for expression.

Themed Meeting Rooms - Enhancing Focus and Encouraging Playful Thinking

"Dazzling Discussion Chambers" unfolds as the fifth chapter, showcasing how businesses are transforming meeting rooms into themed discussion chambers that enhance focus and encourage playful thinking. Meetings are no longer confined to generic boardrooms; they are evolving into dynamic spaces that inspire creativity. Imagine a brainstorming room with walls adorned with vibrant murals that stimulate imaginative thinking or a strategy room with thematic installations that align with the goals of the discussion. Themed meeting rooms become environments that transport participants into different creative realms, enhancing the quality of discussions and encouraging playful approaches to problem-solving.

The transformative impact of dazzling discussion chambers lies in their ability to create memorable and engaging meeting experiences. When employees step into a themed meeting room, it sparks curiosity and sets the stage for innovative thinking. Businesses are recognizing that these creative spaces not only enhance the quality of discussions but also contribute to a workplace culture that values inventive approaches and playful collaboration.

Rotating Art Exhibits - Keeping Playfulness Fresh and Exciting

Conclude our exploration with "Keeping Playfulness Fresh and Exciting," the final chapter that emphasizes the value of rotating art exhibits in office spaces. Businesses recognize that maintaining a playful atmosphere requires ongoing creativity. Imagine an office that features rotating art exhibits, showcasing different artists, styles, and themes throughout the year. Rotating art exhibits ensure that the workplace remains a dynamic and ever-changing canvas, preventing monotony and infusing continuous excitement into the work environment.

The beauty of rotating art exhibits lies in their ability to surprise and delight employees. When the office space evolves with new artworks regularly, it creates an atmosphere of constant discovery. As businesses embrace the concept of rotating art exhibits, they ensure that playfulness remains an integral part of the workplace culture, sparking inspiration and fostering a sense of wonder among employees.

Queue Chromatics: Elevating Customer Experience Through Artful Waiting

Waiting Canvas

Step into the world of queue chromatics, where the waiting experience transforms into a canvas of artistic engagement. This blog post explores the creative potential of incorporating art into queues and lines, enhancing customer experience and turning the often-dreaded waiting time into a delightful and memorable journey.

The Art of Anticipation - Setting the Stage for Positive Waiting

The journey begins with the art of anticipation, strategically designed to set a positive tone for the waiting experience. Engage customers' senses with visually appealing displays, ambient music, and interactive elements that create a sense of excitement and curiosity. Consider using digital screens to showcase dynamic content, such as trivia, entertaining videos, or previews of what's to come. This not only distracts customers from the wait but also fosters a positive and anticipatory mindset.

The art of anticipation extends beyond visuals. Introduce pleasant scents or offer small, themed amenities to create a multisensory experience. By transforming the waiting area into a prelude of the upcoming experience, you turn the art of anticipation into a strategic tool for enhancing customer satisfaction.

Interactive Art Stations - Turning Lines into Creative Hubs

Enter the realm of interactive art stations, where lines become creative hubs of engagement. Instead of mindlessly staring at smartphones, customers can actively participate in art-related activities. Install touchscreen kiosks with drawing apps, puzzles, or collaborative digital art projects. This not only makes waiting more enjoyable but also fosters a sense of community as customers contribute to shared creations.

Consider rotating themes for interactive art stations to keep the experience fresh and engaging. Whether it's a digital coloring book, a collaborative mural, or a quick art quiz, these stations turn waiting time into an opportunity for creativity and connection. By transforming lines into interactive art spaces, you create a dynamic waiting experience that customers will remember and appreciate.

Queue Galleries - Turning Walls into Storytelling Canvases

Queue galleries unfold as a narrative, turning walls into storytelling canvases that captivate and entertain. Display themed art installations or photographs that tell the story of the brand, showcase its history, or highlight customer testimonials. This not only enriches the waiting environment but also reinforces brand identity and values. Consider incorporating QR codes that link to additional information or behind-the-scenes content, providing an interactive element to the gallery experience.

Rotate the exhibits periodically to keep customers engaged and curious about what's coming next. Queue galleries become a seamless blend of art and storytelling, creating an immersive waiting experience that not only entertains but also deepens the connection between customers and the brand.

Artful Distractions - Making Time Fly in the Waiting Game

In the waiting game, artful distractions emerge as the solution to making time fly. Introduce strategically placed distractions, such as optical illusions, interactive mirrors, or even playful sculptures. These elements not only add a touch of whimsy to the waiting area but also serve as conversation starters among customers. Consider incorporating elements that surprise and delight, making the waiting time feel shorter and more enjoyable.

Artful distractions can also include mobile games, AR experiences, or interactive displays that customers can explore while waiting. By infusing the waiting area with elements that engage and entertain, you create a positive and memorable experience that extends beyond the actual service or event.

Queue Symphony - Harmonizing Waiting with Live Performances

Introducing the queue symphony, where live performances harmonize waiting with the magic of the arts. Consider hosting live music performances, small theatrical acts, or even pop-up art installations. This not only creates a dynamic and ever-changing atmosphere but also elevates the waiting experience to a form of entertainment. Queue symphonies foster a sense of enjoyment and appreciation, turning waiting into an integral part of the overall experience.

Collaborate with local artists or performers to bring a touch of the community into the waiting area. The queue symphony becomes an extension of the brand's commitment to creating positive and enriching experiences for its customers. By transforming lines into stages, you turn waiting into an opportunity for customers to be delighted and inspired.

Queue Zen - Creating Tranquil Spaces for Reflection

As the final stroke on the canvas of queue chromatics, the queue zen section introduces tranquil spaces for reflection. Design waiting areas with calming art installations, comfortable seating, and greenery to create a peaceful oasis amidst the hustle and bustle. Consider incorporating elements like water features, soothing music, or even guided meditation sessions to provide customers with a moment of relaxation and mindfulness.

Queue zen areas serve as a sanctuary for customers, allowing them to decompress and reset before their turn comes. By acknowledging the value of customers' time and well-being, queue zen spaces contribute to an overall positive waiting experience that leaves a lasting impression.

Artful Wellness: Designing Holistic Health Spaces with a Brushstroke of Tranquility

The Symphony of Wellbeing - How Art Transforms Health Spaces

Step into the world of "Artful Wellness," where the fusion of art and holistic health spaces creates a symphony of tranquility. In this exploration, we'll uncover the transformative power of integrating art into physical and mental wellbeing environments. From medical facilities to wellness centers, discover how art becomes a healing force, elevating the atmosphere and contributing to the overall wellbeing of individuals seeking solace and recovery.

Healing Murals and Mosaics - A Canvas for Recovery

In "Healing Murals and Mosaics," we dive into the therapeutic impact of large-scale artworks in health spaces. Hospitals and clinics are moving beyond sterile environments, incorporating murals and mosaics that evoke calmness and positivity. Whether it's serene landscapes, vibrant abstracts, or nature-inspired motifs, these artistic expressions become a visual balm for patients, transforming clinical spaces into havens of healing.

The transformative power of healing murals and mosaics lies in their ability to create a calming atmosphere conducive to recovery. Studies suggest that exposure to art can reduce stress, anxiety, and even the perception of pain. By adorning health spaces with aesthetically pleasing visuals, these environments become not just places of treatment but sanctuaries of healing.

Sculpting Serenity - Integrating 3D Art for Spatial Harmony

Explore "Sculpting Serenity," where we delve into the integration of three-dimensional art to enhance spatial harmony in wellness environments. Beyond traditional flat canvases, sculptures and installations bring a tactile and immersive quality to health spaces. Whether it's abstract sculptures in waiting areas or interactive installations in therapy rooms, the use of 3D art engages patients on a sensory level, contributing to an overall sense of tranquility.

The transformative power of sculpting serenity lies in its ability to make health spaces more than clinical settings—they become curated environments that prioritize the mental and emotional aspects of healing. The tactile nature of sculptures provides patients with a multisensory experience, fostering a deeper connection to their surroundings and promoting a sense of calmness.

Mindful Movement - Artful Spaces for Physical Activity

In "Mindful Movement," we explore how art is integrated into spaces designed for physical activity and rehabilitation. Wellness centers and gyms are incorporating artful elements to create motivating environments. From murals that inspire to kinetic sculptures that move with the rhythm of exercise, these artful additions not only make spaces visually appealing but also contribute to the holistic experience of physical wellness.

The transformative power of mindful movement lies in its ability to turn physical activity into a holistic and enjoyable endeavor. Artful spaces encourage individuals to engage in exercise with a sense of purpose and joy, promoting overall physical and mental wellbeing. Businesses in the fitness and wellness industry recognize that this marriage of art and exercise isn't just about aesthetics; it's about creating environments that inspire and invigorate.

Ambient Harmony - The Role of Color Psychology in Wellbeing Spaces

Step into "Ambient Harmony," where we explore the use of color psychology to enhance the therapeutic environment. From waiting rooms to treatment areas, the strategic use of colors in art and decor influences mood and emotions. Soft, soothing hues promote relaxation, while vibrant tones can evoke energy and positivity. By understanding the impact of color on mental states, health spaces are creating atmospheres that contribute to a sense of comfort and emotional balance.

The transformative power of ambient harmony lies in its ability to shape the emotional experience of individuals within health spaces. Colors have a profound impact on mood, and by infusing wellness environments with intentional color choices, these spaces become nurturing and supportive. The recognition of the psychological impact of color is transforming health spaces into places where the mind, body, and spirit find harmony.

Interactive Art Therapy - Nurturing Mental Wellbeing through Expression

In "Interactive Art Therapy," we uncover how mental health spaces are integrating art as a form of therapy. From expressive art workshops to interactive installations that encourage creative expression, mental health facilities are recognizing the healing potential of artistic engagement. Patients are provided with opportunities to use art as a means of communication, self-reflection, and emotional release, contributing to their overall mental wellbeing.

The transformative power of interactive art therapy lies in its ability to empower individuals to express themselves in ways words often cannot. Art becomes a medium for processing emotions, reducing stress, and fostering a sense of agency. Mental health professionals understand that integrating art into therapy isn't just a creative endeavor; it's a powerful tool for promoting self-discovery and emotional healing.

Creating Sanctuaries - Integrating Nature-Inspired Art for Wellbeing

Conclude our exploration with "Creating Sanctuaries," where we delve into the integration of nature-inspired art to create therapeutic sanctuaries. Health spaces are incorporating murals, sculptures, and installations that mimic natural elements, bringing the outdoors inside. Whether it's a calming forest mural in a meditation room or a water-inspired sculpture in a wellness center, nature-inspired art contributes to creating spaces that evoke a sense of tranquility and connection to the natural world.

The transformative power of creating sanctuaries lies in the ability to provide individuals with a respite from the demands of daily life. Nature-inspired art not only enhances the aesthetic appeal of health spaces but also taps into the biophilic connection, fostering a sense of calmness and rejuvenation. Businesses in the health and wellness industry recognize that these sanctuaries aren't just physical spaces; they are integral components of the healing journey.

Creativity Unleashed: Elevating Workspaces with Art Stations for Employee Empowerment

The Canvas of Workplace Creativity

Embark on a journey into the vibrant world where workplace creativity takes center stage, adorned with strategic art stations that empower employees. In this blog post, we delve into the transformative power of art in the workplace, exploring how art stations become catalysts for enhancing employee creativity. Discover the harmonious blend of artistic expression and professional productivity as we unravel the secrets of elevating workspaces through strategic art installations.

Art Stations Unveiled - Crafting Spaces for Creative Expression

Art stations unveiled mark the first step in transforming workplaces into havens for creative expression. Designate specific areas within the office as art stations, complete with a variety of artistic materials and tools. From sketch pads and paints to digital drawing tablets, these stations are curated to cater to diverse creative preferences. The freedom to engage in artistic activities provides employees with a valuable outlet for self-expression and a welcomed break from routine tasks.

Consider the installation of adjustable lighting and comfortable seating to create an inviting atmosphere conducive to creativity. Art stations unveiled not only encourage employees to explore their artistic talents but also foster a sense of autonomy and ownership over their workspace. By incorporating dedicated areas for creative expression, workplaces set the stage for a culture that values and prioritizes the empowerment of employee creativity.

The Strategic Art Gallery - Enhancing Aesthetics and Inspiration

Enter the realm of the strategic art gallery, where workplaces become visually stimulating environments designed to enhance aesthetics and inspiration. Strategic art installations strategically placed throughout the office captivate the senses and spark creativity. Whether it's vibrant murals, thought-provoking sculptures, or interactive digital displays, these installations serve as constant sources of inspiration for employees.

Strategic art galleries should align with the overall aesthetic of the workplace while introducing elements that provoke thought and ignite creativity. Consider rotating installations to keep the environment dynamic, ensuring that employees are continually exposed to fresh and inspiring artistic expressions. The strategic art gallery transforms the workplace into a dynamic, ever-evolving canvas that fuels the imagination and invigorates the creative spirit of the employees.

Artistic Spaces Unleashed - Fostering Collaboration and Ideation

Artistic spaces unleashed become the catalysts for fostering collaboration and ideation within the workplace. Designate areas where employees can engage in collaborative art projects, encouraging them to share ideas and work together on artistic endeavors. These spaces go beyond individual expression, promoting a sense of community and shared creativity among team members.

Consider incorporating collaborative art walls or communal projects that evolve over time, reflecting the collective creativity of the workforce. Artistic spaces unleashed not only enhance teamwork but also serve as tangible representations of the organization's commitment to fostering a collaborative and innovative culture. By providing spaces where employees can collectively unleash their creativity, workplaces become hubs of inspiration and cooperation.

Interactive Art Stations - Infusing Playfulness into Productivity

Interactive art stations emerge as dynamic elements that infuse playfulness into the daily fabric of productivity. Integrate stations where employees can engage in interactive and playful art activities, such as digital art games, kinetic sculptures, or collaborative digital drawing boards. These stations serve as effective stress-relievers, offering moments of creative play that contribute to a positive and energized work environment.

Consider organizing team-building activities around interactive art stations, promoting camaraderie and enhancing interpersonal relationships. The integration of these stations into the workplace ensures that creativity becomes an integral part of the daily routine, contributing to a culture where playfulness and productivity coexist harmoniously.

Holistic Creativity Spaces - Nurturing Mind, Body, and Spirit

Holistic creativity spaces unfold as workplaces recognize the importance of nurturing the holistic well-being of employees. Design areas that integrate art, nature, and relaxation to create holistic creativity spaces. Incorporate indoor plants, natural light, and comfortable seating alongside art stations, providing employees with environments that nurture their minds, bodies, and spirits.

Consider offering mindfulness activities such as guided art meditation or yoga in these spaces to further promote relaxation and mental clarity. Holistic creativity spaces become retreats within the workplace, offering employees the opportunity to recharge and rejuvenate their creativity in an environment that prioritizes their overall well-being.

Employee-Driven Art Initiatives - Cultivating a Culture of Creativity

As the final stroke on the canvas of workplace creativity, employee-driven art initiatives empower individuals to contribute to the artistic narrative of the organization. Encourage employees to propose and lead art projects, exhibitions, or workshops that align with their interests and creative passions. By fostering a culture where employees actively drive artistic initiatives, workplaces become dynamic ecosystems where creativity is not only encouraged but actively cultivated.

Consider establishing an employee art committee that collaborates with management to curate and implement creative initiatives. Employee-driven art initiatives not only contribute to the vibrancy of the workplace but also empower individuals to take ownership of their creative contributions. In doing so, workplaces become not only spaces of employment but thriving communities where creativity is celebrated and nurtured.

Beyond Boardrooms: Creative Wall Art Ideas for Meeting Spaces

Welcome to a realm where creativity and collaboration converge! In "Beyond Boardrooms," we embark on an inspiring journey to revolutionize your meeting spaces with innovative and aesthetic wall art ideas. Elevate your meeting room experience from mundane to extraordinary, fostering a dynamic environment that sparks innovation and enhances communication.

The Power Wall: Igniting Inspiration

In "The Power Wall," discover the potential of creating an impactful focal point that serves as a visual catalyst for ideas and discussions. Explore the use of motivational quotes, graphics, and dynamic imagery that resonate with your company's ethos, motivating teams to approach challenges with enthusiasm.

Consider incorporating a writable surface on the power wall for spontaneous brainstorming sessions, allowing ideas to flow freely.

Themed Nooks: Breaking Monotony with Purpose

Delve into "Themed Nooks" and break away from the monotony of traditional meeting spaces. Explore the concept of creating themed corners within the room, each with its unique art style or color scheme. From nature-inspired havens to futuristic zones, discover how themed nooks can inspire fresh perspectives and fuel creativity during meetings.

Consider involving teams in the selection of themes, ensuring a diverse and inclusive representation of interests.

Interactive Murals: Unleashing Collaborative Creativity

In this section, we unravel the magic of "Interactive Murals." Witness how blank walls transform into collaborative canvases during meetings, encouraging team members to contribute their thoughts visually. Explore the potential of murals that evolve over time, capturing the essence of various projects and milestones.

Consider designating a dedicated mural wall for ongoing projects, creating a living timeline of your team's achievements.

The Digital Canvas: Integrating Technology for Impact

Explore "The Digital Canvas" and discover how technology seamlessly integrates with art in meeting spaces. From interactive displays to digital art installations, learn how incorporating digital elements can enhance presentations, encourage engagement, and bring a futuristic flair to your boardroom.

Consider investing in touchscreen displays that allow team members to interact with digital content during presentations, fostering a dynamic and engaging experience.

Artful Acoustics: Sound-absorbing Wall Installations

Dive into "Artful Acoustics" and explore the intersection of functionality and aesthetics. Discover how sound-absorbing wall installations can mitigate noise levels in meeting spaces while doubling as captivating pieces of art. Uncover innovative materials and designs that enhance both the visual and auditory experience.

Consider commissioning custom acoustic panels featuring patterns or imagery that align with your company's branding.

Lighting Perspectives: Illuminating Ideas with Art

Our final destination, "Lighting Perspectives," explores the transformative power of lighting in meeting spaces. Learn how strategically placed lighting can accentuate artwork, create ambiance, and influence the mood during discussions. From spotlighting key pieces to incorporating LED features, discover how lighting can be an art form in itself.

Consider using smart lighting systems that allow you to customize the ambiance based on the nature of your meetings, whether they're brainstorming sessions or formal presentations.

In Conclusion:

In "Beyond Boardrooms: Creative Wall Art Ideas for Meeting Spaces," we've navigated the exciting realm where art and collaboration intersect. Elevate your meeting spaces to new heights, fostering an environment that nurtures creativity, innovation, and effective communication. Redefine the way your teams engage, ideate, and create within the walls of your meeting rooms.

Productivity Paradise: Elevating Workspaces with the Magic of Creative Décor

Welcome to "Productivity Paradise," where the alchemy of art and creative décor transforms mundane workspaces into vibrant hubs of inspiration and productivity. In this blog post, we explore the profound impact of artistic elements on work environments, unraveling the secrets of curating a space that not only stimulates creativity but also enhances overall productivity. Join us on this journey to discover how the magic of creative décor can turn your workspace into a haven of inspiration.

The Artistic Office Oasis: A Productivity Primer

In "The Artistic Office Oasis," we lay the foundation for a productivity paradise by understanding the principles that make art a catalyst for creativity. Dive into the psychology of colors, the impact of visuals on mood, and the role of creative elements in fostering a positive and energetic atmosphere. Discover how the right combination of colors, patterns, and art pieces can set the tone for a dynamic and inspiring workspace.

Consider incorporating vibrant and uplifting art pieces, such as abstract paintings or nature-inspired prints, to infuse your office with positive energy. The artistic office oasis serves as a primer for creating a conducive environment that sparks creativity and productivity in the blink of an eye.

Curating Creativity: Choosing Art for Focus and Inspiration

Transition into "Curating Creativity," where we guide you through the process of choosing art that enhances focus and inspiration. Explore the concept of thematic decor that aligns with your work objectives and personal preferences. Whether you're drawn to motivational quotes, serene landscapes, or abstract expressions, curating creativity involves selecting art that resonates with your goals and keeps you motivated throughout the day.

Consider creating a gallery wall with a mix of inspirational quotes and visually appealing art to ignite your creativity. By strategically placing these pieces in your line of sight, you'll find yourself effortlessly drawn into a world of focus and inspiration, transforming your workspace into a visual masterpiece.

Beyond the Cubicle: Artful Office Arrangements

Move on to "Beyond the Cubicle," where we break free from the monotony of traditional office setups. Explore innovative ways to arrange art in your workspace, such as incorporating wall decals, desk sculptures, or even a themed corner. Beyond the cubicle, your office space becomes a canvas for self-expression, allowing you to infuse your personality and artistic taste into every nook and cranny.

Experiment with the arrangement of art to create a visually dynamic workspace that fuels your creativity and inspires fresh perspectives. By stepping beyond the confines of a standard cubicle, you open the door to a world of artistic possibilities that enhance both your workspace and your overall sense of well-being.

Personalized Productivity: Customizing Art for Your Workspace

Enter "Personalized Productivity," where we explore the benefits of customizing art to reflect your unique style and preferences. Personalized art has the power to create a sense of ownership and belonging in your workspace, fostering a connection between your environment and your personal aspirations. Dive into the world of custom prints, bespoke artworks, or even DIY projects that reflect your individuality.

Consider commissioning artwork that speaks to your

professional journey, incorporating elements that motivate and inspire you. The personalized productivity approach transforms your workspace into a reflection of your identity, fostering a deeper connection to your work and enhancing your overall sense of fulfillment.

Artful Ergonomics: Merging Comfort and Creativity

In "Artful Ergonomics," we explore the marriage of comfort and creativity in the workplace. Discover how ergonomic furniture, coupled with strategically placed art, contributes to a holistic and artful work environment. From aesthetically pleasing desk accessories to comfortable seating arrangements, the fusion of artful ergonomics creates a workspace that not only enhances productivity but also nurtures your well-being.

Consider investing in ergonomic furniture that complements the aesthetic of your chosen art pieces. The artful ergonomics approach transforms your workspace into a haven where comfort meets creativity, ensuring that your physical and mental well-being are prioritized throughout your workday.

The Power of Breaks: Artful Retreat Spaces

In the final section, "The Power of Breaks," we emphasize the importance of designated retreat spaces within your workspace. Explore how artful retreat spaces, adorned with comfortable seating and inspiring art, can become sanctuaries for rejuvenation and creativity during breaks. From cozy reading corners to vibrant lounges, these retreat spaces offer a refreshing escape from the demands of the workday.

Consider incorporating art that aligns with the theme of your retreat space, creating a cohesive and inviting atmosphere. The power of breaks, enriched by artful retreat spaces, ensures that you recharge your creative energies, fostering a continuous cycle of productivity and inspiration.

Conclusion:

As we conclude our exploration of elevating workspaces with the magic of creative décor in "Productivity Paradise," remember that art has the extraordinary ability to transform your work environment into a haven of inspiration. Whether you're curating creativity, breaking free from the cubicle, embracing personalized productivity, merging artful ergonomics, or discovering the power of breaks, each section unveils a facet of the transformative power that art and creative décor hold in enhancing your overall productivity.

Brushing Success: Unveiling the Psychology of Color in Business Wall Art

A Palette of Possibilities

Welcome to the vibrant world of business wall art, where colors aren't just hues but strategic tools for success. In the realm of design, the psychology of color plays a pivotal role, influencing emotions, behaviors, and perceptions. This blog post dives deep into the artful science of color, exploring how businesses can leverage it strategically in their wall art to create an environment that not only stimulates but captivates. So, let's embark on this chromatic journey together.

Color Me Productive - Boosting Office Morale with Wall Art

Imagine walking into an office adorned with a sea of cool blues and greens. The calming effect of these colors isn't just coincidence; it's a deliberate choice. Blue is associated with productivity and focus, while green promotes a sense of calm and balance. Strategic use of these hues in business wall art can significantly impact employee morale and performance. Studies have shown that the right colors in the workplace can reduce stress, enhance concentration, and foster a positive work environment.

When selecting wall art for the office, consider the nature of the work and the atmosphere you want to cultivate. For collaborative spaces, opt for energizing colors like yellow and orange to foster creativity and communication. In private offices, choose calming tones like lavender or muted blues to promote concentration. By using color strategically, businesses can create a workspace that not only looks good but also nurtures a conducive environment for success.

Branding Brilliance - Communicating Identity Through Color

In the competitive world of business, branding is everything. Your brand colors are more than just a visual identity; they are a powerful communication tool. Integrating these colors into your office wall art can reinforce brand recognition and create a cohesive visual experience for clients and employees alike. If your brand exudes trust and reliability, incorporate blues and grays into your office art. For a more energetic and dynamic brand, reds and yellows might be the way to go.

Consistency is key. Ensure that the colors in your wall art align with your brand palette. This not only strengthens your brand identity but also contributes to a professional and polished aesthetic. When clients walk into your office, the colors on the walls should resonate with the colors in your logo, creating a harmonious visual symphony that speaks volumes about your brand personality.

The Subtle Influencer - Color's Impact on Customer Perception

In the retail world, the strategic use of color can be a game-changer. The right colors in your wall art can influence customer perception, behavior, and even purchasing decisions. Warm tones like red and orange are known to stimulate appetite, making them ideal for restaurants or food-related businesses. Cool tones like blues and greens convey a sense of calm and trust, perfect for creating a serene shopping experience.

Color can also guide customers through a space. Accent walls in strategic colors can draw attention to specific areas or products. For example, a vibrant red wall can highlight a sale or promotion, while a soothing green wall can lead customers to a tranquil lounge area. By understanding the psychology of color, businesses can curate a shopping environment that not only attracts but also engages customers on a subconscious level.

The Power of Contrast - Making a Statement with Color Combinations

In the world of design, contrast is a powerful tool. When it comes to business wall art, the strategic use of color combinations can make a bold statement. High-contrast color schemes, like black and white or complementary colors, can create a visually striking and memorable space. Contrast draws the eye and can be used to highlight specific elements, such as a company logo or a featured product.

Consider the mood you want to evoke. A high-energy startup might opt for bold contrasts like black and red, while a sophisticated law firm might lean towards classic contrasts like navy and gold. Don't be afraid to experiment with unexpected color pairings – it can add a touch of creativity and uniqueness to your space. By playing with contrast, businesses can turn their walls into dynamic canvases that tell a story and leave a lasting impression.

Beyond the Basics - Incorporating Accent Colors with Purpose

While the overall color scheme sets the tone, accent colors add depth and personality to your business wall art. These are the pops of color that catch the eye and create visual interest. Think of accent colors as the accessories that complete an outfit. Whether it's a vibrant piece of artwork, a colorful mural, or even strategically placed plants, accents can elevate the entire aesthetic of your space.

Choose accent colors that complement your overall scheme but also inject a sense of vibrancy. If your office is primarily neutral, a burst of yellow or orange can infuse energy. For a more muted palette, consider accents in jewel tones for a touch of sophistication. Accent colors should be used sparingly to avoid overwhelming the space, but when done right, they can add a layer of depth and personality that sets your business apart.

The Ever-Evolving Canvas - Adapting Colors to Trends and Seasons

The world of design is ever-evolving, and so should your business wall art. Stay attuned to color trends and consider refreshing your wall art to reflect the current zeitgeist. Pantone's Color of the Year is a good indicator of upcoming trends and can offer inspiration for a timely update. Seasonal changes also present opportunities to inject new life into your space. Warm, earthy tones for fall and cool, icy hues for winter can create a dynamic and ever-changing visual experience for clients and employees alike.

Adapting your wall art to trends doesn't necessarily mean

a complete overhaul. Small updates, like changing accent pieces or incorporating seasonal art prints, can make a significant impact. This flexibility not only keeps your space visually engaging but also communicates that your business is dynamic, forward-thinking, and always in tune with the times.

In Conclusion: Painting Success, One Wall at a Time

In the canvas of business, color is the brushstroke that paints success. From boosting office morale to influencing customer perception, the strategic use of hues in business wall art is an art and a science. By understanding the psychology of color, businesses can create environments that not only look aesthetically pleasing but also serve as powerful tools for communication, branding, and engagement. So, embrace the palette of possibilities, and let your walls tell a story of success in every shade.

Healing Horizons: Crafting Artful Designs for Holistic Wellness Centers

The Art of Healing - Redefining Spaces for Holistic Wellness

Step into the world of "Healing Horizons," where the fusion of art and design transforms holistic wellness centers into sanctuaries of healing. In this exploration, we unveil the artful designs that breathe life into these spaces, creating environments that nurture the mind, body, and spirit. From soothing aesthetics to purposeful layouts, discover how holistic wellness centers are redefining the art of healing through intentional and thoughtful design.

1: The Serenity of Entrance - A Prelude to Tranquility

In "The Serenity of Entrance," we delve into the importance of the first impression in holistic wellness centers. The entrance sets the tone for the entire healing experience, and artful design plays a pivotal role in creating an immediate sense of calmness and serenity. From carefully curated artwork to nature-inspired decor, the entrance becomes a prelude to the tranquility that awaits within.

The transformative power of the serenity of entrance lies in its ability to initiate a shift in mindset. As visitors step into the wellness center, the intentional design communicates a message of peace and healing. Holistic wellness centers recognize that this initial impression isn't just about aesthetics; it's about creating an atmosphere that invites individuals to leave the stresses of the outside world behind and enter a space dedicated to their wellbeing.

2: Mindful Layouts - Navigating Spaces with Intention

Explore "Mindful Layouts," where we uncover how holistic wellness centers utilize intentional designs to create spaces that guide individuals on their healing journey. From the arrangement of treatment rooms to the flow of communal areas, the layout of the center is crafted with purpose. Artful design ensures that each space serves a specific function, fostering a sense of order and mindfulness.

The transformative power of mindful layouts lies in their ability to enhance the overall experience of individuals seeking wellness. When spaces are thoughtfully arranged, it contributes to a seamless and stress-free journey through the center. Holistic wellness centers recognize that this intentional design isn't just about aesthetics; it's about creating an environment where individuals can easily navigate, promoting a sense of security and relaxation.

3: Nature-Inspired Retreats - Bringing the Outdoors In

In "Nature-Inspired Retreats," we explore the incorporation of natural elements in the design of holistic wellness centers. From indoor gardens to nature-inspired artwork, these retreats bring the healing power of the outdoors inside. The integration of natural elements not only adds visual appeal but also contributes to a sense of connection with the environment, promoting overall wellbeing.

The transformative power of nature-inspired retreats lies in their ability to create spaces that resonate with individuals on a deep level. When the healing qualities of nature are brought into the design, it adds a layer of authenticity to the wellness experience. Holistic wellness centers recognize that this connection with nature isn't just about aesthetics; it's about creating environments that align with the principles of holistic healing.

4: Calming Treatment Rooms - A Canvas for Healing

Step into "Calming Treatment Rooms," where we explore how the design of individual treatment spaces becomes a canvas for healing. These rooms are carefully curated to evoke a sense of calmness and relaxation. From muted color palettes to strategically placed artwork, the design of treatment rooms plays a crucial role in creating an environment that supports the healing process.

The transformative power of calming treatment rooms lies in their ability to enhance the effectiveness of therapeutic interventions. When individuals enter these spaces, the intentional design sets the stage for a focused and tranquil healing experience. Holistic wellness centers recognize that this attention to detail isn't just about aesthetics; it's about creating treatment rooms that are conducive to the physical, mental, and emotional aspects of healing.

5: Community Connection Spaces - Fostering Supportive Environments

In "Community Connection Spaces," we uncover how holistic wellness centers design communal areas to foster a sense of community and support. From cozy lounges to shared gardens, these spaces are crafted with the intention of promoting connection and a sense of belonging. Artful design in communal areas encourages individuals to come together, share experiences, and build a supportive community.

The transformative power of community connection spaces lies in their ability to create a holistic wellness ecosystem. When individuals feel connected to a community that shares similar wellness goals, it contributes to a sense of accountability and motivation. Holistic wellness centers recognize that these communal spaces aren't just about aesthetics; they're about creating environments that encourage individuals to embark on their healing journeys together.

6: Integrating Technology for Holistic Healing - A Modern Approach

Conclude our exploration with "Integrating Technology for Holistic Healing," where we delve into how holistic wellness centers embrace modern technology to enhance the healing experience. From interactive displays that provide educational content to virtual wellness programs, technology is seamlessly integrated to complement traditional healing practices. The artful design ensures that technology enhances, rather than detracts from, the overall sense of tranquility and mindfulness.

The transformative power of integrating technology for holistic healing lies in its ability to make wellness practices more accessible and engaging. When technology is thoughtfully integrated into the design, it becomes a tool for empowerment and education. Holistic wellness centers recognize that this marriage of technology and design isn't just about keeping up with the times; it's about leveraging advancements to make holistic healing more inclusive and effective.

Café Culture: Elevating Hospitality Spaces with Unique Wall Décor

Step into the enchanting world of "Café Culture: Elevating Hospitality Spaces with Unique Wall Décor," where every sip of coffee is accompanied by a visual feast. In this blog post, we explore the symbiotic relationship between cafés and captivating wall décor, unraveling the secrets behind creating a cozy, inviting atmosphere. From quirky murals to eclectic gallery walls, join us on a journey through the art-infused realms of cafés that go beyond just serving coffee.

Artistic Brews: The Marriage of Coffee and Creativity

In "Artistic Brews," we delve into the magical fusion of coffee and creativity. Explore how café owners are transforming their spaces into veritable art galleries, showcasing the work of local artists or commissioning bespoke pieces that reflect the unique personality of their establishment. Discover the power of art to enhance the coffee-drinking experience, creating a harmonious blend of taste and visual delight.

Consider partnering with local artists or incorporating art pieces that resonate with your café's theme, turning every cup of coffee into a multisensory experience.

Mural Magic: Transforming Walls into Artistic Canvases

Uncover the enchantment of "Mural Magic" as we explore how murals are turning café walls into captivating canvases. From whimsical scenes to abstract expressions, witness the transformative impact of large-scale murals on the ambiance of a café. Learn from establishments that have embraced mural art, turning their walls into iconic landmarks that draw in patrons and encourage social media sharing.

Consider commissioning a mural that reflects the essence of your café, creating a visual landmark that becomes synonymous with your brand.

Gallery Gastronomy: Culinary Art Meets Visual Art

In "Gallery Gastronomy," we explore the intersection of culinary art and visual art within cafés. Delve into the trend of cafés doubling as art galleries, showcasing not only delectable treats but also curated displays of local artwork. Discover how this fusion of gastronomy and visual aesthetics elevates the overall dining experience, inviting customers to indulge their senses in a feast for both the eyes and the palate.

Consider partnering with local artists for rotating exhibitions, creating an ever-evolving gallery space within your café.

Bohemian Bliss: Creating a Laid-Back Artsy Atmosphere

Explore the "Bohemian Bliss" trend, where cafés are embracing a laid-back, artsy atmosphere. From mismatched furniture to an eclectic mix of wall art, witness how cafés are cultivating an environment that encourages patrons to linger, sip, and soak in the creative vibes. Learn how the bohemian aesthetic contributes to a sense of community and fosters a unique identity for each café.

Consider incorporating bohemian elements into your café's décor, creating a relaxed and inviting space that encourages customers to unwind.

Upcycled Elegance: Sustainable Décor for Eco-Conscious Cafés

In "Upcycled Elegance," we explore the rise of sustainable décor in cafés, where upcycled and repurposed materials are used to create unique wall installations. Dive into the world of eco-conscious cafés that prioritize sustainability without compromising on style. Learn how recycled materials and DIY art projects contribute to a visually appealing and environmentally friendly ambiance.

Consider incorporating upcycled elements into your café's design, aligning with the growing trend of sustainability in the hospitality industry.

Interactive Art Spaces: Engaging Customers in the Creative Process

In "Interactive Art Spaces," discover how cafés are engaging customers in the creative process, turning their establishments into interactive art spaces. From communal chalkboards to DIY art stations, explore the innovative ways cafés are inviting patrons to become a part of the artistic experience. Learn how these interactive elements contribute to a sense of community and make every visit a memorable affair.

Consider implementing interactive art installations that encourage customers to express their creativity, fostering a sense of connection and participation.

Conclusion:

In "Café Culture: Elevating Hospitality Spaces with Unique Wall Décor," we've uncovered the myriad ways in which cafés are using art to create unforgettable experiences. From artistic brews to interactive art spaces, the relationship between cafés and wall décor is a testament to the power of visual aesthetics in enhancing hospitality spaces. Elevate your café into a haven of creativity, where every sip is savored amidst a backdrop of artistic expression.

Hotel Elegance: Elevating Guest Experiences with Luxurious Wall Art

Welcome to a world where opulence meets artistic expression – "Hotel Elegance." In this blog post, we'll explore the transformative power of luxurious wall art in creating an atmosphere of refinement and sophistication, ensuring an unforgettable experience for hotel guests. From grand lobbies to intimate suites, discover how carefully curated art can elevate the ambiance of luxury hotels.

The Grand Gallery: Making a Statement in Hotel Lobbies

In "The Grand Gallery," we delve into the importance of making a striking first impression in hotel lobbies. Explore how large-scale, statement artworks can set the tone for the entire guest experience. From monumental sculptures to awe-inspiring paintings, discover how these grand pieces contribute to the overall ambiance, creating a sense of luxury and sophistication from the moment guests step through the doors.

Consider commissioning a signature art piece that reflects the hotel's unique identity and captivates guests as they enter the lobby.

Suite Retreat: Tailoring Art to Guest Accommodations

In "Suite Retreat," we explore the art of tailoring wall art to guest accommodations. Learn how hotels are personalizing suites with curated art collections that align with the overall design aesthetic. From custom-made headboards to carefully selected paintings, discover how attention to detail in guest rooms enhances the overall sense of luxury and comfort.

Consider collaborating with local artists to create exclusive, limited-edition art pieces for each suite, providing guests with a truly unique and immersive experience.

Culinary Canvases: Art in Hotel Dining Spaces

In "Culinary Canvases," we savor the integration of art in hotel dining spaces. Explore how luxurious wall art enhances the dining experience, creating an ambiance that complements the culinary delights. From elegant paintings to innovative installations, discover how the fusion of art and gastronomy elevates the overall enjoyment of fine dining.

Consider selecting art that harmonizes with the restaurant's theme and cuisine, creating a visual feast for guests to savor.

Spa Serenity: Creating Tranquil Environments with Art

In "Spa Serenity," we unwind in the tranquil embrace of luxurious spas adorned with carefully chosen wall art. Explore the use of soothing colors, nature-inspired artworks, and serene sculptures to create an atmosphere of relaxation and rejuvenation. Learn how art contributes to the overall wellness experience, transforming spa spaces into havens of serenity.

Consider incorporating nature-themed art pieces in spa areas to enhance the connection between guests and the natural elements.

Timeless Treasures: Incorporating Art in Historic Hotel Spaces

In "Timeless Treasures," we explore the art of preserving history while infusing contemporary luxury in historic hotel spaces. Discover how carefully selected artworks can complement the architectural heritage of the building while adding a touch of modern elegance. From curated galleries to art-inspired tours, learn how hotels are embracing their past while looking towards the future.

Consider partnering with local historical societies or art institutions to create curated exhibits that celebrate the hotel's rich history.

Event Elegance: Art as a Centerpiece in Hotel Events

In "Event Elegance," we spotlight the role of art as a centerpiece in hotel events. Explore how curated art installations and live art experiences can elevate the ambiance of conferences, weddings, and social gatherings. Learn about the impact of art in creating memorable moments and enhancing the overall guest experience during special events.

Consider offering art-inspired event packages that include curated installations and live art performances, providing a unique and memorable experience for event attendees.

In Conclusion:

In "Hotel Elegance: Elevating Guest Experiences with Luxurious Wall Art," we've explored the multifaceted ways in which art contributes to the ambiance of luxury hotels. From grand lobbies to intimate suites, culinary spaces, spas, historic areas, and events, carefully curated art plays a pivotal role in creating an environment that resonates with sophistication and indulgence.

Walls Alive: The Marvels of Office Murals Transforming Corporate Spaces

Brushing Corporate Drabness Away

Step into the vibrant world of office murals, where creativity knows no bounds, and corporate interiors become canvases for artistic expression. This blog post explores the transformative power of large-scale office murals, diving into the ways they can breathe life into corporate spaces, boost employee morale, and redefine the very essence of office aesthetics.

The Grand Introduction - Setting the Stage for Office Murals

Office murals are not just decorative elements; they're transformative experiences that begin the moment you step through the door. The grand introduction of an office mural sets the stage for a shift in the corporate atmosphere. Large-scale art has the ability to make a bold statement about a company's values, culture, and creative spirit. It becomes a visual representation of the brand, leaving a lasting impression on employees, clients, and visitors alike.

Consider commissioning a mural that encapsulates the essence of your company – its mission, vision, or core values. This grand introduction serves as a visual handshake, welcoming everyone into a space where creativity and innovation are not just encouraged but celebrated.

Employee Engagement Canvas - Boosting Morale Through Art

Office murals go beyond aesthetics; they play a crucial role in shaping the employee experience. A well-crafted mural can be a powerful tool for boosting morale, fostering a positive work environment, and instilling a sense of pride among employees. The engagement canvas created by an office mural becomes a daily source of inspiration, motivating employees to bring their best selves to work.

Consider involving employees in the mural creation process, whether through brainstorming sessions, collaborative workshops, or even allowing them to contribute to the artwork. This participatory approach not only strengthens the sense of ownership but also ensures that the mural resonates with the diverse perspectives within the workforce. The result is a workplace adorned with a mural that reflects the collective spirit of the team.

Dynamic Workspaces - Redefining Corporate Interiors with Murals

Corporate interiors are often synonymous with neutrality, but office murals have the power to redefine these spaces. Break away from the monotony of bland walls and introduce dynamic workspaces that inspire and invigorate. Murals can transform meeting rooms, hallways, and even break areas into visually stimulating environments, promoting creativity and a sense of identity within the workplace.

Consider themes that align with the function of each space. For collaborative areas, opt for vibrant and energetic murals that encourage teamwork and innovation. In relaxation zones, choose calming and abstract designs that provide a respite from the demands of the workday. By strategically placing murals throughout the corporate interiors, you create a dynamic and purposeful environment that speaks to the varied needs of employees.

Beyond Aesthetics - Murals as Storytelling Tools

Office murals are more than just aesthetically pleasing; they are powerful storytelling tools. Through visuals, murals can narrate the history, achievements, and aspirations of a company. Whether showcasing milestones, depicting the journey of growth, or highlighting key moments in the corporate timeline, murals turn walls into dynamic storyboards that communicate the narrative of the business.

Consider collaborating with artists who specialize in storytelling through visual elements. Murals can depict the evolution of the company, paying homage to its roots while looking towards the future. This storytelling aspect not only adds depth to the corporate culture but also creates a sense of continuity, connecting past successes to present efforts.

Branding Beyond Logos - Murals as Brand Identity Statements

Move beyond the limitations of logos and taglines – office murals can serve as comprehensive brand identity statements. Incorporate brand colors, values, and unique visual elements into the mural design. This holistic approach to branding creates a cohesive and immersive experience for both employees and visitors, reinforcing brand recognition and leaving a lasting imprint.

Consider murals that seamlessly blend the visual language of the brand with the ethos of the company. Whether it's abstract representations of brand values or literal interpretations of products and services, murals become an integral part of the brand's physical identity. The result is a corporate space where every inch resonates with the essence of the brand.

A Legacy of Creativity - The Timelessness of Office Murals

Unlike fleeting trends, office murals have the potential to become timeless features within corporate spaces. While the business world evolves, the murals stand as testaments to creativity, innovation, and the unique identity of the company. Invest in murals that have a lasting impact, both in terms of craftsmanship and relevance to the brand, ensuring that they continue to inspire and captivate for years to come.

Consider murals that transcend temporary aesthetics and tap into universal themes or timeless design principles. This timeless quality ensures that the murals remain relevant, regardless of changing trends or shifts in the corporate landscape. As a legacy of creativity, office murals become a constant source of inspiration and a symbol of the enduring spirit of the company.

Brushing Away Stress: Artful Strategies for Workplace Wellness

A Stroke of Wellness

In the hustle and bustle of the modern workplace, employee well-being is taking center stage. Beyond traditional wellness programs, companies are turning to the world of art to foster a healthier and more vibrant work environment. This blog post delves into the transformative power of art in the workplace, exploring how it can alleviate stress, boost creativity, and contribute to overall employee wellness.

The Healing Canvas - Art's Impact on Stress Reduction

The stressors of daily work life can take a toll on employees, affecting their mental and physical health. Incorporating art into the workplace acts as a therapeutic intervention, offering employees a visual escape from the demands of their tasks. Studies have shown that exposure to art, whether through paintings, sculptures, or installations, can reduce stress levels and promote relaxation.

Consider creating designated art spaces within the office, where employees can take short breaks to engage with art. These areas can be adorned with calming paintings, greenery, or even interactive art installations. The act of immersing oneself in art provides a mental reset, fostering a sense of calm that can have lasting effects on stress management.

Colorful Cubicles - The Impact of Personalized Workspaces

Empower your employees to turn their workspaces into personal art galleries. Allowing individuals to personalize their desks or cubicles with art that resonates with them can enhance their emotional connection to the workspace. Encourage the display of artwork, family photos, or even motivational quotes. This not only adds a splash of color to the office but also creates a positive and uplifting atmosphere.

Artistic expression in personal workspaces has been linked to increased job satisfaction and a sense of autonomy. When employees surround themselves with images that inspire and motivate, it can positively influence their mood and mindset throughout the workday. The key is to strike a balance between personalization and maintaining a professional work environment.

Artistic Breaks - Nurturing Creativity and Innovation

In the pursuit of productivity, creativity often takes a backseat. However, incorporating art into the workplace can act as a catalyst for creative thinking. Dedicate specific spaces for artistic breaks or brainstorming sessions, where employees can engage in activities like sketching, painting, or crafting. These breaks not only refresh the mind but also stimulate creative thinking and problem-solving skills.

Consider organizing art workshops or providing art supplies for employees to use during breaks. The act of creating art activates different areas of the brain, promoting divergent thinking and fostering a more innovative workplace culture. By nurturing creativity through art, companies can unlock untapped potential within their teams.

Team-Building Murals - Fostering Collaboration Through Art

Art has the power to bring people together and foster a sense of community. Consider organizing team-building activities that involve collaborative art projects. Large murals or installations created by teams can serve as tangible representations of shared goals and values. This not only enhances teamwork but also transforms the workplace into a more visually dynamic and engaging space.

Collaborative art projects promote communication, cooperation, and a sense of collective achievement. They provide a break from the routine and allow employees to connect on a more personal level. The resulting art pieces can be proudly displayed in communal areas, serving as a constant reminder of the collaborative spirit that defines the organization.

Artful Wellness Programs - Integrating Creativity into Health Initiatives

Wellness programs are evolving beyond traditional fitness challenges. Incorporating art into these programs adds a creative dimension to employee health initiatives. Consider organizing art classes, mindfulness sessions through art, or even art therapy workshops. These activities not only contribute to physical well-being but also address mental health, providing employees with a holistic approach to wellness.

Artful wellness programs offer a unique avenue for self-expression and self-discovery. They create a supportive environment where employees can explore their creative side while reaping the benefits of improved mental and emotional well-being. By integrating creativity into wellness initiatives, companies can demonstrate a commitment to the overall health of their workforce.

The Artful Office - A Cultural Shift Towards Employee Well-Being

Transforming the workplace into an artful haven isn't just a trend; it's a cultural shift towards prioritizing employee well-being. The artful office reflects a commitment to creating a positive, inspiring, and inclusive environment. It sends a powerful message that the company values the holistic health of its employees, contributing to higher morale, increased job satisfaction, and ultimately, greater productivity.

In conclusion, the integration of art into the workplace is more than just aesthetic enhancement; it's an investment in the well-being and success of the workforce. Whether through stress reduction, personalized workspaces, creative breaks, collaborative projects, or innovative wellness programs, the artful workplace paves the way for a brighter, healthier, and more fulfilling professional journey.

Entrance Elegance: Elevating First Impressions with Lobby Statements

The Grand Overture - Making a Statement in Business Lobbies

Embark on a journey into the world of "Entrance Elegance," where the power of impactful wall art transforms business lobbies into captivating spaces that leave a lasting impression. In this blog post, we'll explore the art of making a statement in lobbies, welcoming visitors with a visual symphony that sets the tone for their entire experience. From bold murals to carefully curated galleries, discover how businesses are turning their lobbies into artistic canvases that speak volumes without uttering a word.

The Power of First Impressions - Crafting Memorable Welcomes

Begin our exploration with "Crafting Memorable Welcomes," the first chapter that delves into the significance of first impressions in business lobbies. The lobby is the overture of a visitor's experience, and the right wall art can orchestrate a welcoming melody. Imagine a corporate office with a striking mural reflecting the company's ethos or a hotel lobby adorned with a carefully curated art gallery. Crafting memorable welcomes through impactful wall art not only captures attention but also sets a positive and lasting tone for visitors.

The transformative power of first impressions lies in their

ability to shape perceptions. When visitors are greeted by impactful wall art that resonates with the identity of the business, it becomes a visual handshake, fostering a sense of connection and professionalism. Businesses recognize that this intentional crafting of welcomes goes beyond aesthetics; it becomes a strategic tool for creating positive associations from the very first moment.

Murals that Speak Volumes - Visual Narratives in Business Lobbies

Dive into the second chapter, "Visual Narratives in Business Lobbies," where we explore how businesses are using murals as powerful storytelling tools in their lobbies. Murals go beyond mere decoration; they become visual narratives that convey the essence and values of the company. Picture a technology company with a mural depicting the evolution of innovation or a healthcare facility with a mural celebrating the human spirit. Murals that speak volumes not only engage visitors visually but also communicate the identity and purpose of the business in a language that transcends words.

The transformative impact of visual narratives lies in their ability to create a sense of connection and resonance. When visitors encounter a mural that tells a story, it transforms the lobby into more than just a waiting area; it becomes a space where they can immerse themselves in the narrative of the business. Businesses recognize that these murals serve as powerful ambassadors, conveying messages and fostering a deeper understanding of the organization.

Gallery Showcases - Elevating Lobbies into Artistic Sanctuaries

"Elevating Lobbies into Artistic Sanctuaries" unfolds as the third chapter, showcasing how businesses are transforming lobbies into curated gallery showcases. Lobbies aren't merely transitional spaces; they become artistic sanctuaries that engage and inspire. Imagine a corporate headquarters with rotating art exhibits or a law firm with a gallery showcasing the intersection of art and justice. Gallery showcases not only add aesthetic value but also create dynamic and ever-evolving environments that captivate and intrigue visitors.

The transformative impact of artistic sanctuaries lies in their ability to foster a sense of exploration and appreciation. When visitors step into a lobby that resembles a curated gallery, it elevates the entire experience, encouraging them to engage with the artworks and the space itself. Businesses recognize that these gallery showcases not only reflect a commitment to creativity but also create a memorable and sophisticated ambiance that distinguishes their lobby from the ordinary.

Interactive Installations - Engaging Visitors Beyond the Surface

Enter the realm of "Engaging Visitors Beyond the Surface," the fourth chapter that explores how businesses are incorporating interactive installations to deepen visitor engagement in lobbies. Wall art isn't limited to being observed; it becomes an interactive experience that invites visitors to actively participate. Picture a corporate lobby with a digital art installation that responds to touch or a hotel lobby with an interactive display allowing guests to create their own digital art. Interactive installations not only break the barrier between observer and art but also turn the lobby into a space of exploration and hands-on engagement.

The transformative impact of interactive installations lies in their ability to turn lobbies into dynamic and participatory environments. When visitors can actively engage with the art, whether through touch, motion, or contribution, it transforms the lobby into a space where they become part of the creative experience. Businesses recognize that these interactive elements not only add layers of interest but also contribute to a sense of connection and memorable experiences that linger in the minds of visitors.

Sculptural Elegance - Three-Dimensional Statements in Lobbies

"Sculptural Statements in Lobbies" unfolds as the fifth chapter, showcasing how businesses are incorporating three-dimensional sculptures to make bold statements in their lobbies. Sculptures go beyond the flat surface, adding depth, texture, and a touch of elegance. Imagine a law firm with a sculpture embodying the scales of justice or a corporate lobby adorned with abstract sculptures representing innovation and collaboration. Sculptural statements not only capture attention but also become iconic focal points that embody the values and identity of the business.

The transformative impact of sculptural elegance lies in its ability to create a sense of permanence and distinction. When visitors encounter sculptural statements in lobbies, it goes beyond fleeting impressions; it becomes a tangible and enduring symbol of the business. Businesses recognize that these three-dimensional artworks not only add a touch of sophistication but also contribute to a sense of legacy and identity that lingers in the memories of visitors.

The Continuity of Experience - Extending Impact Beyond the Lobby

Conclude our exploration with "Extending Impact Beyond

the Lobby," the final chapter that emphasizes how businesses are strategically extending the impact of lobby statements beyond the entrance. The lobby isn't an isolated space; it's the starting point of a journey. Imagine a corporate office with thematic art installations that continue into meeting rooms or a hotel lobby with curated art pathways leading to different amenities. The continuity of experience not only ensures that the impact of lobby statements lingers but also creates a seamless and immersive journey for visitors.

The transformative power of extending impact lies in its ability to create a cohesive and integrated experience. When visitors move beyond the lobby and encounter a continuation of the artistic narrative, it reinforces the initial impressions and contributes to a sense of consistency and purpose. Businesses recognize that this strategic extension ensures that the impact of lobby statements permeates every aspect of the visitor experience, creating a holistic and memorable journey.

Branding with Art: Using Wall Decor to Reinforce Company Identity

Welcome to a world where art meets business, and creativity intertwines with corporate identity. In this blog post, we'll explore the fascinating realm of "Branding with Art" and how strategically chosen wall decor can become a powerful tool in reinforcing your company's unique identity.

1. Setting the Stage: The Impact of Art in Corporate Spaces

The first section, "Setting the Stage," delves into the transformative impact of art in corporate spaces. Discover how the carefully curated art on your office walls can set the tone for visitors and employees alike, creating an environment that reflects your company's ethos. From vibrant abstracts to industry-specific themes, explore the art of making a lasting impression from the moment someone steps into your space.

Consider incorporating your brand colors and values into the artwork, creating a visual representation of your company's personality.

2. Beyond Logos: Expressing Brand Personality in Art

In "Beyond Logos," we explore how wall decor can go beyond mere logos, becoming a dynamic expression of your brand's personality. Dive into the world of custom art that encapsulates your company culture, values, and mission. Learn how this personalized approach to wall decor can create a deeper connection with both clients and employees, making your workspace a true reflection of who you are.

Consider involving employees in art-related activities to foster a sense of ownership and connection to the company identity.

3. Thematic Narratives: Telling Your Company Story through Art

"Thematic Narratives" uncovers the storytelling potential of wall decor. Discover how thematic art displays can narrate your company's journey, milestones, and achievements. From a visual timeline on your office walls to art that embodies your brand's evolution, explore the art of telling your company story through the language of visuals.

Consider commissioning artists to create pieces that depict significant moments in your company's history, fostering a sense of pride and connection among employees.

4. Branded Spaces: Integrating Art into Your Branding Strategy

"Branded Spaces" takes a deep dive into the concept of integrating art seamlessly into your branding strategy. Explore how your office spaces can become an extension of your brand, creating a cohesive visual language that resonates with clients and reinforces your corporate identity. From conference rooms to common areas, learn how to infuse every corner with the essence of your brand.

Consider collaborating with local artists or art studios to create unique pieces that reflect your brand values and resonate with the local community.

5. Employee Engagement: Fostering a Sense of Belonging through Art

In "Employee Engagement," we explore how art can contribute to fostering a sense of belonging and unity among your team. Learn how art-related initiatives, such as employee art showcases or collaborative mural projects, can enhance teamwork and strengthen the bond between employees and your company. Discover the art of creating a workspace where every team member feels connected to the brand they represent.

Consider organizing art-related team-building activities to encourage collaboration and creativity among employees.

6. Future-Proofing Brand Identity: Adapting Art to Evolving Narratives

Our final section, "Future-Proofing Brand Identity," focuses on the dynamic nature of corporate narratives. Explore strategies for adapting your wall art to evolving brand stories, ensuring that your company's identity remains relevant and resonant over time. Discover how art can be a flexible and powerful tool for expressing the ever-evolving spirit of your brand.

Consider implementing a rotating art program to regularly refresh your office spaces with new pieces that align with your current brand narrative.

Conclusion:

In "Branding with Art: Using Wall Decor to Reinforce Company Identity," we've embarked on a journey to uncover the myriad ways art can become an integral part of your brand strategy. From making a powerful first impression to fostering employee engagement, let this blog post inspire you to view wall decor not just as embellishments but as essential elements in shaping and reinforcing your company's unique identity.

Retail Therapy: Using Art to Enhance the Shopping Experience

Welcome to "Retail Therapy: Using Art to Enhance the Shopping Experience," where we embark on a journey through the creative and captivating world of retail design. In this blog post, we explore how the strategic use of art can transform a shopping space into a haven for sensory delight, elevating the overall retail experience. From innovative store layouts to art-infused visual merchandising, discover the secrets to creating a shopping environment that leaves a lasting impression.

Artful Entrances: Setting the Tone for a Unique Shopping Adventure

In "Artful Entrances," we delve into the importance of the first impression in retail. Explore how the entrance of a store can be a powerful canvas for artistic expression, setting the tone for the entire shopping experience. Discover examples of businesses that have crafted memorable entrances, using art installations, dynamic lighting, and captivating displays to draw customers into the world of their brand.

Consider incorporating eye-catching art elements near entrances, creating a visual prelude to the retail journey that awaits inside.

Visual Merchandising Magic: Art as a Sales Catalyst

Uncover the magic of "Visual Merchandising" as we explore how art serves as a catalyst for sales. Dive into the world of strategic visual merchandising, where art plays a pivotal role in creating compelling product displays. Learn from retail giants that have mastered the art of arranging merchandise in a way that not only showcases products but also tells a story, invoking emotions that drive purchasing decisions.

Consider experimenting with artful displays that complement your product offerings, transforming the act of shopping into a visually engaging and emotionally resonant experience.

Thematic Territories: Using Art to Define Retail Spaces

In "Thematic Territories," we discuss how art can be used to define different zones within a retail space. Explore the concept of thematic retailing, where distinct sections of a store are infused with art that complements specific product categories. Learn from retailers who have successfully created thematic territories, enhancing the overall shopping experience by immersing customers in carefully curated environments.

Consider incorporating art installations or murals that visually guide customers through different retail zones, making the shopping journey more enjoyable and memorable.

Interactive Installations: Turning Shopping into an Artistic Experience

In "Interactive Installations," discover the transformative power of art in making shopping a truly artistic experience. Explore how retailers are incorporating interactive art installations that engage customers on a sensory level. From digital displays to hands-on installations, learn how these artistic elements are turning shopping into a dynamic and immersive adventure.

Consider integrating interactive art elements that invite customers to participate actively in the shopping experience, creating memorable moments that extend beyond the transaction.

Artful Ambiance: Enhancing the Shopping Atmosphere

Explore the impact of "Artful Ambiance" on the overall shopping atmosphere. Delve into the use of art to create a sensory-rich environment that goes beyond product displays. Discover how lighting, music, and carefully chosen art pieces contribute to a welcoming and enjoyable ambiance, influencing the way customers perceive and interact with a retail space.

Consider incorporating ambient art elements, such as sculptures or wall murals, to enhance the overall atmosphere and create a space where customers feel comfortable and inspired.

Artful Branding: Infusing Brand Identity into Retail Spaces

In "Artful Branding," we explore how art can be a potent tool for infusing brand identity into retail spaces. Understand the role of art in communicating brand values, personality, and story. Learn from businesses that have successfully used art to create a cohesive brand narrative throughout their retail locations, fostering a deeper connection with customers.

Consider commissioning custom art pieces that reflect your brand's ethos, weaving a unique artistic thread that ties all your retail spaces together.

Conclusion:

In "Retail Therapy: Using Art to Enhance the Shopping Experience," we've unraveled the secrets to creating a shopping environment that transcends the transactional. Elevate your retail space into a haven of artful delight, where every corner tells a story, and every display is a visual masterpiece. From thematic territories to interactive installations, discover how the strategic infusion of art can turn a shopping trip into an unforgettable experience.

Artistry Unveiled: Transforming Conference Spaces with Unique Centerpieces

The Canvas of Conferences

Embark on a journey into the world of artistry unveiled, where conference spaces become canvases waiting to be adorned with unique centerpieces. In this blog post, we explore the profound impact of art in event spaces, specifically focusing on the transformative power of conference centerpieces. Discover how these artistic focal points can elevate the atmosphere, engage attendees, and leave a lasting impression on the overall conference experience.

1: The Artful Prelude - Setting the Tone for Conference Magic

The artful prelude sets the stage for conference magic, establishing the tone and atmosphere from the moment attendees enter the space. Centerpieces serve as the first brushstrokes on this canvas, capturing attention and signaling that this is not just another conference but an immersive and visually stimulating experience. Consider centerpieces that align with the conference theme, incorporating elements that resonate with the event's purpose and message.

Whether it's a dynamic sculpture representing innovation or

a floral arrangement mirroring the company's brand colors, the artful prelude creates a sense of anticipation and curiosity among attendees. These centerpieces become conversation starters, sparking interactions and setting a positive and engaging tone for the conference ahead.

2: Theme Fusion - Aligning Centerpieces with Conference Narratives

Enter the world of theme fusion, where centerpieces seamlessly align with the conference narratives and objectives. Centerpieces should go beyond mere decoration; they should tell a story. Whether the conference focuses on technology, sustainability, or industry trends, the centerpieces become visual elements that reinforce and amplify the event's key messages.

Consider collaborating with artists or designers who can create custom centerpieces that embody the essence of the conference theme. From abstract installations to interactive displays, theme fusion ensures that every centerpiece contributes to the overall narrative, creating a cohesive and immersive experience for attendees. These themed centerpieces serve as visual anchors, grounding attendees in the conference's purpose and reinforcing key takeaways.

3: Interactive Elegance - Engaging Attendees Beyond the Surface

Interactive elegance takes centerpieces beyond the realm of static decoration, encouraging attendee engagement and participation. Incorporate elements that invite interaction, whether it's a digital display with touch sensors, a collaborative art installation, or even a centerpiece that doubles as a charging station for electronic devices. These interactive features not only capture attention but also create memorable moments that attendees can actively be a part of.

Consider incorporating gamification elements into centerpieces, turning them into challenges or quizzes related to the conference content. This not only adds an element of fun but also ensures that attendees are actively engaging with the event's key messages. Interactive elegance transforms centerpieces into dynamic focal points that go beyond aesthetics, enhancing the overall conference experience.

4: Sustainable Statements - Eco-Friendly Centerpieces with Impact

In the era of sustainability, centerpieces become powerful tools for making eco-friendly statements. Consider opting for sustainable materials, such as recycled paper, biodegradable elements, or even potted plants that can be taken home by attendees after the conference. These sustainable centerpieces not only contribute to reducing environmental impact but also showcase the conference's commitment to responsible practices.

Collaborate with local artisans or eco-friendly suppliers to create centerpieces that align with the conference's sustainability goals. From upcycled sculptures to living centerpieces that promote green initiatives, sustainable statements ensure that every aspect of the conference, including the centerpieces, reflects the organization's dedication to a greener and more responsible future.

5: Artistic Networking - Centerpieces as Conversation Catalysts

Artistic networking unfolds as centerpieces take on the role of conversation catalysts, encouraging attendees to connect and engage. Create centerpieces that are not just visually appealing but also serve a functional purpose. For example, opt for table centerpieces that incorporate discussion prompts or conversation cards related to conference topics. This prompts meaningful interactions among attendees and facilitates networking in a natural and artful manner.

Consider incorporating elements like communal art projects or collaborative displays that encourage attendees to contribute and engage with one another. Artistic networking transforms centerpieces into dynamic hubs of connection, fostering a sense of community among conference participants. These centerpieces become more than just visual adornments; they become active facilitators of relationship-building and idea exchange.

6: The Lasting Impression - Centerpieces Beyond the Conference Walls

As the final brushstroke on the canvas of artistry unveiled, centerpieces have the power to leave a lasting impression that extends beyond the conference walls. Consider offering attendees the opportunity to take home elements of the centerpieces or transforming them into branded merchandise. Whether it's a mini version of a thematic sculpture or a potted plant from a sustainable centerpiece, these tangible takeaways ensure that the impact of the conference continues long after the event concludes.

Photograph the centerpieces and share them on social media platforms, creating a digital footprint that extends the reach of the conference. The lasting impression of centerpieces goes beyond their physical presence, becoming a visual legacy that reinforces the positive memories and key messages of the conference.

Wall Art in Vacation Homes: Elevating the Rental Property Experience

Artful Escapes - The Power of Wall Decor in Vacation Rentals

Embark on a journey with "Wall Art in Vacation Homes: Elevating the Rental Property Experience" as we explore how thoughtfully curated wall art can transform a temporary dwelling into a memorable escape. Discover the nuances of creating an artful ambiance that enchants guests and keeps them coming back for more.

"The Welcome Canvas: First Impressions Matter"

In "The Welcome Canvas," uncover the significance of creating a captivating first impression through carefully chosen wall art. Delve into the psychology of guest expectations and learn how strategically placed artwork sets the stage for a delightful vacation experience from the moment they step through the door.

"Local Flavor on Display: Connecting Guests with the Destination"

Explore the concept of "Local Flavor on Display," where we discuss the artful integration of local artwork to create a sense of place. Discover how showcasing regional artists or incorporating elements of the destination's culture through wall decor enhances the overall guest experience, fostering a connection between visitors and the locale.

"Creating Ambiance: The Art of Theme-Based Decor"

In "Creating Ambiance," unravel the art of theme-based decor that transforms vacation homes into thematic retreats. Learn how selecting wall art that complements the overall design theme - whether it be coastal, rustic, or contemporary - contributes to a cohesive and immersive atmosphere that resonates with guests.

"Art for Comfort: Making Spaces Feel Like Home"

Delve into "Art for Comfort" as we explore how well-chosen wall art contributes to the homely feel of vacation rentals. Discover the subtle ways in which artwork can enhance comfort, creating a welcoming environment that encourages relaxation and allows guests to fully unwind during their stay.

"Insta-Worthy Spaces: The Social Media Influence of Artful Interiors"

Uncover the significance of "Insta-Worthy Spaces" and the impact of visually appealing interiors on social media engagement. Explore how vacation homes adorned with eye-catching wall art become shareable havens, attracting attention on social platforms and generating organic marketing for property owners.

"Practical Considerations: Durability, Maintenance, and Flexibility"

Conclude our journey with "Practical Considerations," addressing the importance of durability, maintenance, and flexibility in selecting wall art for vacation homes. Learn how to strike a balance between aesthetics and practicality, ensuring that the chosen decor withstands the wear and tear of regular guest turnover.

Retail Storyscapes: Artful Journeys Guiding Customers Through the Space

Crafting Narratives with Canvas - The Art of Retail Storyscapes

Welcome to "Retail Storyscapes," where the canvas of retail spaces transforms into immersive environments, telling captivating stories through carefully curated art. In this exploration, we delve into the world of retail story arcs, where art takes center stage to guide customers through a curated journey. From captivating entrances to themed sections, discover how retailers are using art as a powerful tool to create unique and memorable shopping experiences, captivating customers from the moment they step through the door.

The Grand Overture - Creating Impactful Entrances with Artful Statements

In "The Grand Overture," we explore the importance of creating impactful entrances that set the stage for the retail story arc. This section discusses how retailers use artful statements, whether through large-scale sculptures, dynamic installations, or bold signage, to capture the attention of customers from the very beginning. Discover how the grand overture transforms entrances into visual spectacles that not only welcome customers but also hint at the narrative that awaits them within the store.

The transformative power of the grand overture lies in its

ability to create a sense of anticipation and excitement. When retailers invest in making entrances visually stunning, it sets the tone for a unique shopping experience. Businesses recognize that the grand overture isn't just about making a first impression; it's about inviting customers into a world where art becomes an integral part of the retail journey, sparking curiosity and engagement.

Thematic Realms - Guiding Customers Through Curated Sections

Step into "Thematic Realms," where we explore how retailers use art to guide customers through curated sections that tell distinct parts of the overall story. This section discusses the concept of thematic realms, where each section of the store is designed with a specific theme, color palette, or artistic style. Discover how retailers strategically use art to create transitions between these realms, offering customers a seamless and visually captivating journey as they explore different facets of the store.

The transformative power of thematic realms lies in their ability to turn the retail space into a narrative-driven environment. When retailers curate sections with specific themes and connect them through artful transitions, it elevates the overall shopping experience. Businesses recognize that thematic realms aren't just about organizing products; they're about immersing customers in a cohesive story that keeps them engaged and encourages exploration.

Artful Signposts - Navigating Retail Story Arcs with Visual Cues

In "Artful Signposts," we explore the importance of using visual cues and signage as navigational tools within the retail space. This section discusses how retailers strategically place art installations as signposts, guiding customers through the different chapters of the retail story arc. From interactive installations that provide information to sculptures that serve as landmarks, discover how artful signposts enhance wayfinding and contribute to a seamless and enjoyable shopping experience.

The transformative power of artful signposts lies in their ability to simplify navigation and enhance the overall customer journey. When retailers use art as a wayfinding tool, it adds an extra layer of engagement and makes the shopping experience more memorable. Businesses recognize that artful signposts aren't just about directing traffic; they're about creating a visually appealing and intuitive path that encourages customers to explore and discover.

Temporal Tales - Rotating Art Installations for Dynamic Experiences

Explore "Temporal Tales," where we delve into the concept of rotating art installations that bring dynamism to the retail story arc. This section discusses how retailers use temporary art exhibits, seasonal displays, or rotating installations to keep the narrative fresh and exciting. Discover how temporal tales inject a sense of novelty and urgency, encouraging customers to return regularly to experience new chapters of the story and discover the latest artistic expressions.

The transformative power of temporal tales lies in their ability to create a sense of anticipation and exclusivity. When retailers introduce rotating art installations, it adds an element of surprise and keeps the retail space evolving. Businesses recognize that temporal tales aren't just about changing aesthetics; they're about creating a dynamic and ever-changing environment that fosters customer loyalty and repeat visits.

Interactive Epilogues - Engaging Customers in the Closing Chapters

In "Interactive Epilogues," we explore how retailers use interactive art installations as epilogues that engage customers in the closing chapters of their shopping journey. This section discusses the concept of interactive exhibits, where customers can participate in creating art or experiencing immersive installations. Discover how interactive epilogues not only serve as memorable closing moments but also encourage customers to share their experiences, becoming part of the narrative that extends beyond the store.

The transformative power of interactive epilogues lies in their ability to turn customers into active participants in the retail story arc. When retailers create opportunities for engagement through interactive art, it enhances the emotional connection customers have with the brand. Businesses recognize that interactive epilogues aren't just about closing the shopping experience; they're about turning customers into brand advocates who share their unique and participatory experiences with others.

Customer-Centric Narratives - Adapting Retail Story Arcs to Individual Journeys

Conclude our exploration with "Customer-Centric Narratives," where we discuss the importance of adapting retail story arcs to cater to individual customer journeys. This section explores how retailers can use data and customer feedback to personalize the retail story, ensuring that each shopper's experience feels tailored and unique. Discover how customer-centric narratives create a sense of belonging, encouraging customers to see the retail space as a canvas for their own stories and preferences.

The transformative power of customer-centric narratives lies in their ability to create a sense of inclusivity and personalization. When retailers adapt their story arcs to align with individual customer preferences, it fosters a deeper connection and loyalty. Businesses recognize that customer-centric narratives aren't just about telling a single story; they're about creating a flexible and adaptive narrative that evolves with the diverse needs and preferences of their customer base.

Dynamic Designs: Wall Art for Modern and Trendy Workspaces

Welcome to the vibrant world of "Dynamic Designs," where we explore the intersection of art and modern workspaces. In this blog post, we'll delve into the transformative power of wall art in creating trendy, dynamic, and inspiring environments that cater to the needs of contemporary professionals.

Setting the Tone: The Impact of Wall Art on Workspace Atmosphere

In "Setting the Tone," we unravel the profound influence of wall art on shaping the atmosphere of modern workspaces. From calming abstracts to energizing geometric patterns, discover how the right art pieces can set the mood, enhance creativity, and contribute to a positive and productive environment. Learn about the psychological effects of color and form in creating a conducive workspace.

Consider the personality of your team and the nature of your work when selecting art pieces to evoke the desired ambiance.

Beyond Blank Walls: Transformative Murals and Large-scale Installations

In "Beyond Blank Walls," we explore the bold and impactful world of transformative murals and large-scale installations. Discover how artists and designers are pushing the boundaries of traditional wall art, turning entire walls into immersive experiences. Learn about the trend of custom murals that reflect company values, brand identity, and inspire creativity among employees.

Consider collaborating with local artists to create a bespoke mural that tells your company's story and invigorates your workspace.

Digital Frontier: Integrating Technology and Art in Modern Offices

In "Digital Frontier," we dive into the synergy between technology and art, exploring how digital displays, interactive installations, and augmented reality are redefining the modern workspace. Learn about the practical applications of digital art in creating dynamic and adaptive office environments that resonate with the tech-savvy workforce.

Consider incorporating digital art displays that can be easily updated to keep the workspace dynamic and aligned with your brand messaging.

Artistic Workstations: Elevating Individual Spaces with Personalized Art

In "Artistic Workstations," we explore the trend of personalizing individual workspaces with curated art. Discover how employees are embracing self-expression through the art they choose to surround themselves with. Learn about the positive impact of personalized workstations on employee well-being, creativity, and job satisfaction.

Consider encouraging employees to bring their artistic touch to their workspaces, fostering a sense of ownership and individuality.

Curated Collections: Building Art Galleries within the Office

In "Curated Collections," we unravel the concept of creating mini art galleries within office spaces. Explore how curated art collections can tell a visual story, reflect the company's values, and stimulate conversation among employees. Learn about the curation process and how diverse art selections can cater to a broad range of tastes and preferences.

Consider working with an art curator to assemble a collection that aligns with your company culture and inspires creativity.

Sustainable Aesthetics: Eco-Friendly Art for Modern Workspaces

In "Sustainable Aesthetics," we explore the rising trend of incorporating eco-friendly and sustainable art in modern workspaces. Discover how recycled materials, upcycled art, and pieces with environmentally conscious themes can contribute to a green and responsible office design. Learn about the positive impact of sustainable aesthetics on employee morale and corporate social responsibility.

Consider sourcing art from local artists who specialize in sustainable and eco-friendly creations, aligning with your commitment to environmental consciousness.

Conclusion:

In "Dynamic Designs: Wall Art for Modern and Trendy Workspaces," we've embarked on a journey through the diverse and exciting ways art can transform the modern workplace. By embracing dynamic designs, companies can foster creativity, boost employee morale, and create environments that resonate with the evolving needs of today's professionals.

Wander, Work, Create: Unveiling Artistic Spaces for Digital Nomad Hubs

The Nomadic Canvas - Where Remote Work Meets Artistic Inspiration

Embark on a journey where the canvas of remote work meets the brushstrokes of artistic inspiration in "Wander, Work, Create." In this exploration, we uncover the dynamic world of Digital Nomad Hubs, where workspaces transcend the traditional, embracing artful designs that not only facilitate productivity but also foster creativity and collaboration among remote professionals. From vibrant coworking spaces to collaborative art installations, discover how these hubs are redefining the landscape of remote work.

Nomadic Nests - Crafting Inviting Coworking Spaces

In "Nomadic Nests," we delve into the vibrant and inviting coworking spaces that serve as the beating heart of digital nomad hubs. These spaces are more than just desks and chairs; they are carefully curated environments that balance productivity with comfort. From eclectic decor to flexible workstations, the design of these nomadic nests encourages collaboration and a sense of community among individuals on their remote work journey.

The transformative power of nomadic nests lies in their ability to transform workspaces into dynamic hubs of creativity. When remote professionals step into these coworking spaces, the intentional design sets the stage for a productive and inspiring workday. Digital nomad hubs recognize that these spaces aren't just about functionality; they're about creating environments that inspire and energize individuals pursuing their professional endeavors.

Mural Moments - Transforming Walls into Storytelling Canvases

Explore "Mural Moments," where we unravel how digital nomad hubs transform blank walls into vibrant storytelling canvases. Murals and street art become an integral part of the hub's identity, reflecting the spirit of the community and the local culture. These artistic expressions not only add visual appeal but also serve as conversation starters, fostering connections and a sense of belonging among the diverse individuals who pass through these nomadic spaces.

The transformative power of mural moments lies in their ability to create a unique and immersive atmosphere within digital nomad hubs. When walls become canvases for artistic expression, it adds a layer of inspiration to the work environment. Digital nomad hubs recognize that these murals aren't just about decoration; they're about creating spaces that tell stories, spark conversations, and contribute to a shared sense of identity.

Collaborative Corners - Where Ideas Converge and Flourish

In "Collaborative Corners," we uncover the carefully

designed spaces within digital nomad hubs that encourage collaboration and idea sharing. These corners go beyond traditional meeting rooms, offering informal meeting spots, brainstorming areas, and project collaboration zones. The intentional design fosters an environment where remote professionals can come together, exchange ideas, and embark on collaborative ventures that transcend geographical boundaries.

The transformative power of collaborative corners lies in their ability to break down the barriers of remote work, fostering a sense of teamwork and camaraderie. When individuals have dedicated spaces for collaboration, it promotes a culture of innovation and shared success. Digital nomad hubs recognize that these collaborative corners aren't just about convenience; they're about creating spaces that facilitate meaningful connections and the birth of new ideas.

Nature-Inspired Retreats - Green Oasis for Remote Rejuvenation

Step into "Nature-Inspired Retreats," where we explore how digital nomad hubs incorporate green spaces and nature-inspired design elements. From rooftop gardens to indoor plants, these retreats provide remote professionals with areas to unwind, recharge, and connect with the natural world. The integration of nature-inspired design not only enhances the aesthetics of the workspace but also contributes to the overall wellbeing of digital nomads.

The transformative power of nature-inspired retreats lies in their ability to create a holistic work environment that prioritizes the mental and emotional health of remote professionals. When nature becomes an integral part of the design, it adds a refreshing and rejuvenating element to the workday. Digital nomad hubs recognize that these retreats aren't just about aesthetics; they're about creating spaces that promote balance and harmony in the lives of nomadic workers.

Tech-Infused Havens - The Marriage of Innovation and Design

In "Tech-Infused Havens," we unravel how digital nomad hubs seamlessly integrate technology into their design to create innovative workspaces. From smart desks that adjust to individual preferences to virtual reality collaboration spaces, these havens marry cutting-edge technology with intentional design. The result is a workspace where digital nomads can leverage the latest tech advancements to enhance their remote work experience.

The transformative power of tech-infused havens lies in their ability to make remote work more efficient, connected, and enjoyable. When technology is thoughtfully integrated into the design, it becomes a tool for empowerment and productivity. Digital nomad hubs recognize that this marriage of innovation and design isn't just about keeping up with the times; it's about leveraging advancements to create workspaces that are at the forefront of the digital era.

Cultural Catalysts - Nurturing Local Art and Entrepreneurship

Conclude our exploration with "Cultural Catalysts," where we discover how digital nomad hubs become catalysts for local art and entrepreneurship. These hubs embrace the communities they inhabit, showcasing local artists, hosting cultural events, and supporting local businesses. The intentional integration of local culture not only enriches the experience of remote professionals but also contributes to the economic and cultural vibrancy of the surrounding area.

The transformative power of cultural catalysts lies in their ability to create a symbiotic relationship between digital nomads and the local community. When hubs become hubs of cultural exchange, it adds a layer of depth and authenticity to the nomadic experience. Digital nomad hubs recognize that these cultural catalysts aren't just about global connectivity; they're about fostering a sense of belonging and making a positive impact on the places they call home.

Art and Innovation: Fostering Creativity in Tech and Startup Offices

Welcome to the intersection of creativity and innovation in "Art and Innovation: Fostering Creativity in Tech and Startup Offices." In this blog post, we embark on a journey to explore how art can be a catalyst for innovation in the dynamic world of tech and startup environments. From inspiring workspaces to enhancing collaboration, discover the transformative power of art in driving creativity and innovation.

The Creative Nexus: Designing Inspirational Workspaces

In "The Creative Nexus," we delve into the importance of designing inspirational workspaces that stimulate creativity in tech and startup offices. Explore how strategic placement of art, vibrant colors, and unique installations can foster a conducive environment for out-of-the-box thinking. Learn from case studies showcasing companies that have successfully integrated art into their office design to enhance creativity and productivity.

Consider implementing flexible seating arrangements and open spaces adorned with visually stimulating artwork to encourage spontaneous collaboration and idea generation.

Artistic Motivation: Boosting Employee Morale and Productivity

Explore "Artistic Motivation" and uncover how curated art pieces can boost employee morale and overall productivity in tech and startup offices. Understand the psychological impact of art on motivation, engagement, and job satisfaction. Discover innovative approaches to incorporating motivational art that aligns with the fast-paced and dynamic nature of the tech industry.

Consider organizing art-related activities such as team-building art workshops or featuring employee-created artwork to instill a sense of ownership and motivation.

Creative Corners: Establishing Art Hubs for Collaborative Thinking

In "Creative Corners," we highlight the concept of establishing art hubs within offices to promote collaborative thinking. Dive into the benefits of designated creative spaces where employees can engage with art, exchange ideas, and find inspiration. Learn about successful implementations of art hubs in tech and startup environments that have resulted in breakthrough innovations.

Consider allocating specific areas as creative corners, equipped with writable surfaces, interactive displays, and thought-provoking art installations to encourage spontaneous brainstorming sessions.

Tech and Art Fusion: Showcasing Innovation Through Interactive Installations

In "Tech and Art Fusion," discover the fascinating world of interactive installations that showcase innovation and creativity in tech offices. Explore the synergy between technology and art, from augmented reality displays to interactive sculptures. Learn how merging tech and art can create immersive experiences that inspire inventive thinking among employees.

Consider collaborating with local artists or tech innovators to create interactive installations that reflect the cutting-edge spirit of your tech or startup office.

Mindful Creativity: Incorporating Art for Stress Reduction and Focus

In "Mindful Creativity," we explore the role of art in promoting stress reduction and enhancing focus in tech and startup workplaces. Delve into the therapeutic effects of art on the mind and its potential to create a calm and focused atmosphere. Learn about the incorporation of mindfulness practices through art in high-pressure work environments.

Consider incorporating elements like nature-inspired art, calming colors, and designated quiet zones to provide employees with spaces for relaxation and rejuvenation.

Art as a Catalyst: Driving Innovation in Startup Culture

In our final section, "Art as a Catalyst," we examine how art serves as a catalyst for driving innovation in startup culture. Uncover the ways in which embracing art can shape a unique and inspiring company culture, attracting top talent and fostering a spirit of experimentation. Learn from startup success stories that attribute their innovative edge to a culture infused with artistic expression.

Consider organizing regular art exhibitions or installations within your startup, creating a platform for employees to showcase their creative talents and celebrate diversity in innovation.

Conclusion:

In "Art and Innovation: Fostering Creativity in Tech and Startup Offices," we've explored the symbiotic relationship between art and innovation in the fast-paced world of technology. Elevate your office environment to a new realm of creativity, where art not only decorates but also inspires and drives groundbreaking ideas. Transform your tech or startup office into a canvas of innovation, cultivating an atmosphere that nurtures creativity and propels your company into the future.

The Waiting Gallery: Elevating Customer Experience with Art in Waiting Areas

The Artful Prelude to a Positive Experience

Waiting areas are more than transitional spaces; they're the prelude to an experience. Imagine transforming these often mundane spaces into engaging galleries that captivate, relax, and leave a lasting impression. In this blog post, we'll explore the transformative power of art in waiting areas, uncovering how it enhances the customer experience and turns waiting into a delightful part of the journey.

The Canvas of Calm - Creating Serene Waiting Spaces

Waiting rooms are notorious for inducing stress, but art has the magical ability to turn tension into tranquility. Through strategic choices of paintings, sculptures, or even immersive installations, waiting areas can be transformed into serene spaces that put visitors at ease. Active choices of soothing colors and nature-inspired themes can create a calming atmosphere, setting the stage for a positive experience.

Imagine a waiting room adorned with nature landscapes or abstract art that evokes a sense of serenity. Visitors can engage with the artwork, allowing their minds to wander and temporarily escape the stress of waiting. By actively curating a calming visual environment, businesses not only improve the customer experience but also position themselves as considerate and customer-centric.

The Art of Distraction - Turning Waiting into Enjoyable Moments

Waiting is often associated with boredom, but art has the power to transform this perception. Engaging and thought-provoking art installations in waiting areas can act as delightful distractions, turning what might be perceived as wasted time into an enjoyable and enriching experience. Whether it's interactive digital displays or rotating exhibits, businesses can actively involve visitors in the artistic journey.

Active participation can be encouraged through art that invites reflection or prompts interaction. Consider strategically placing sculptures that visitors can touch or digital displays that allow them to create virtual art. By actively choosing art that captivates attention, businesses not only alleviate the feeling of waiting but also create positive memories associated with their brand.

The Conversation Starter - Fostering Connections Through Art

Art has a unique ability to bring people together, and waiting areas can become social hubs through strategic art choices. Engage visitors in conversation by selecting pieces that are visually intriguing and open to interpretation. Abstract art, in particular, can be a fantastic conversation starter, allowing visitors to share their perspectives and connect with one another.

Active facilitation of dialogue through art contributes to a sense of community in waiting areas. Visitors may find common ground in their interpretations of a piece, creating a shared experience that enhances the overall atmosphere. By actively curating art that encourages interaction, businesses not only elevate the waiting experience but also foster a sense of connection among their visitors.

Aesthetic Branding - Crafting a Visual Identity in Waiting Areas

Waiting areas serve as the first physical touchpoint for many customers, making them an ideal canvas for showcasing a brand's aesthetic identity. Actively curating art that aligns with the brand's values, colors, and themes reinforces a cohesive visual identity. This intentional approach extends the brand experience, leaving a lasting impression on visitors and enhancing overall brand recall.

Consider commissioning custom artwork that incorporates elements of the brand logo or color palette. This not only adds a unique touch to the waiting area but also reinforces brand recognition. By actively infusing waiting areas with branded art, businesses create a holistic and immersive brand experience that begins the moment visitors step into the space.

Art as Therapy - Elevating Wellbeing in Waiting Spaces

Waiting areas are ideal spaces for promoting mental wellbeing through carefully selected art. Active choices of pieces that evoke positive emotions, convey uplifting messages, or showcase scenes of beauty can contribute to a therapeutic atmosphere. This is particularly beneficial in healthcare settings where patients may experience anxiety or stress.

Imagine a medical waiting room adorned with art that promotes healing, calmness, and hope. The active integration of therapeutic art not only supports the mental and emotional wellbeing of visitors but also positions the business as empathetic and caring. By actively considering the impact of art on wellbeing, businesses contribute to a positive and supportive waiting environment.

Rotating Exhibits and Fresh Perspectives - Keeping Waiting Areas Dynamic

To keep the waiting experience dynamic, consider introducing rotating art exhibits. This active approach prevents monotony and offers visitors something new to engage with during each visit. Rotating exhibits can feature local artists, thematic displays, or even tie into current events, keeping the waiting area visually stimulating and relevant.

Active planning and curation of rotating exhibits involve collaboration with local artists, art organizations, or in-house creative teams. This not only supports the local arts community but also injects a sense of excitement and anticipation into the waiting experience. By actively embracing change and variety in waiting areas, businesses ensure that visitors are always met with fresh perspectives and engaging visual stimuli.

Transforming the Ordinary into the Extraordinary

In the waiting room, art becomes a powerful tool for transforming the ordinary into the extraordinary. By actively curating a visual environment that soothes, engages, and connects, businesses elevate the customer experience and leave a lasting impression. From calming canvases to dynamic exhibits, the artful touch in waiting areas actively contributes to a positive and memorable journey for every visitor.

Crafting a Professional Image: Choosing Wall Art for Corporate Offices

Welcome to the world where the aesthetics of your office space speak volumes about your professionalism. In this blog post, we'll guide you through the art of "Crafting a Professional Image" by strategically selecting wall art for corporate offices, ensuring your workspace reflects the competence and character of your business.

The Power of First Impressions: Art in the Reception Area

Our journey begins with "The Power of First Impressions." Dive into the importance of the reception area as the first point of contact for clients and visitors. Explore how carefully chosen artwork in this space can set the tone, conveying professionalism, creativity, and a welcoming atmosphere. From large-scale installations to curated galleries, discover the art of making a lasting impression from the moment someone steps through your doors.

Consider incorporating your company's branding colors or motifs into the artwork to reinforce brand identity right from the entrance.

Corporate Culture on Canvas: Reflecting Values in Boardrooms

In "Corporate Culture on Canvas," we explore the role of boardrooms as spaces for critical decision-making and client presentations. Uncover how art in these settings can mirror your company's core values and corporate culture. From abstract pieces that evoke creativity to motivational artwork that inspires, learn how to infuse your boardroom with art that aligns with your business philosophy.

Consider rotating artwork to keep the boardroom environment dynamic and aligned with evolving business objectives.

Employee Well-being: Art in Workspaces for Motivation and Productivity

"Employee Well-being" focuses on the impact of art in individual workspaces. Explore how personalized art choices for employee offices or cubicles can contribute to motivation, creativity, and overall job satisfaction. Discover the art of creating a workspace where employees feel inspired, fostering a positive and productive work environment.

Consider involving employees in the selection of artwork for their individual workspaces, promoting a sense of ownership and personalization.

Navigating Common Areas: Fostering Collaboration with Art

Our fourth section, "Navigating Common Areas," delves into the significance of shared spaces. Learn how to use art to foster collaboration, creativity, and a sense of community in break rooms, lounges, or cafeterias. Explore the potential of murals, sculptures, or interactive installations to create engaging and collaborative environments that bring employees together.

Consider incorporating artwork that reflects the diversity and inclusivity of your company culture in common areas.

Branding Beyond Logos: Using Art to Tell Your Corporate Story

In "Branding Beyond Logos," we explore how art can be a powerful tool for storytelling. Delve into the idea of creating a visual narrative that tells your corporate story through carefully selected pieces. From historical timelines to thematic exhibits, discover how art can be a dynamic and engaging way to communicate your company's journey, achievements, and future aspirations.

Consider commissioning artists to create bespoke pieces that capture the essence of your company's history and future vision.

Sustainability and Art: Making Ethical Choices for Corporate Decor

Our final section, "Sustainability and Art," addresses the growing importance of making ethical choices in corporate decor. Explore how eco-friendly and sustainable art options can contribute to a positive corporate image. From recycled materials to supporting local artists, learn how to align your company with sustainable practices through conscientious choices in wall art.

Consider implementing a corporate art policy that outlines guidelines for sustainable and ethical art choices.

In Conclusion:

In "Crafting a Professional Image: Choosing Wall Art for Corporate Offices," we've explored the nuanced art of creating a workspace that aligns with your business's professional image. From making a powerful first impression to fostering employee well-being and sustainability, let this blog post serve as your guide to curating a corporate environment that speaks volumes about your professionalism and values.

Meeting Marvels: Elevating Conference Room Themes with Artful Inspirations

The Artful Prelude to Productive Meetings

Welcome to the world of Meeting Marvels, where the mundane transforms into the extraordinary through the power of artful conference room themes. In this blog post, we embark on a journey to explore how businesses are using art to set the tone for meetings, turning conference rooms into dynamic spaces that inspire creativity, collaboration, and productivity. From thematic installations to curated wall art, discover the artful inspirations that are reshaping the dynamics of modern meetings.

The Power of First Impressions - Crafting Inviting Entrances

Unlock the first chapter, "Crafting Inviting Entrances," where we delve into the significance of the first impression. The entrance to a conference room sets the stage for the meeting experience. Businesses are leveraging art to create welcoming and visually striking entrances that set a positive tone for discussions. Imagine a conference room with a thematic door mural that hints at the topic of the meeting or a reception area adorned with dynamic sculptures that serve as a prelude to the creative energy within. Crafting inviting entrances is about creating an atmosphere that sparks curiosity and anticipation, setting the foundation for a productive meeting.

The power of first impressions extends beyond aesthetics; it influences the mindset of meeting participants. When individuals step into a conference room and are greeted by thoughtfully curated art, it creates a sense of excitement and engagement. Businesses recognize that the journey into a meeting space is as important as the discussions that follow, and art becomes the tool to craft entrances that leave a lasting impression.

Theming for Purpose - Tailoring Environments to Meeting Goals

Dive into the second chapter, "Tailoring Environments to Meeting Goals," where we explore how businesses are using art to theme conference rooms based on the specific purpose of the meeting. Different meetings have different objectives, and art is becoming a key element in tailoring environments to align with these goals. Imagine a strategy session in a room adorned with motivational quotes and abstract art that stimulates creative thinking or a brainstorming session surrounded by vibrant colors and dynamic installations. Theming for purpose ensures that the environment actively supports the objectives of the meeting, fostering a focused and conducive atmosphere.

The artful integration of thematic elements goes beyond decoration; it becomes a tool for enhancing the effectiveness of discussions. When meeting participants find themselves in a space that resonates with the goals at hand, it creates a sense of cohesion and alignment. Businesses are recognizing the power of theming for purpose as a strategy to elevate the impact of meetings and make the environment an active participant in the collaborative process.

Mood-Setting Murals - Transforming Walls into Inspirational Canvases

"Transforming Walls into Inspirational Canvases" emerges as the third chapter, unveiling how businesses are using murals to set the mood for meetings. Murals have the power to transform ordinary walls into dynamic and inspirational canvases. Picture a conference room with a mural depicting the company's journey or values, creating a backdrop that inspires team members or a project room adorned with a mural that visually represents the objectives and milestones. Mood-setting murals become integral components of the meeting environment, infusing spaces with energy, motivation, and a sense of identity.

The transformative impact of mood-setting murals lies in their ability to actively contribute to the meeting atmosphere. Whether it's fostering a sense of unity, igniting creativity, or reinforcing company culture, murals become visual anchors that guide the emotional tone of discussions. As businesses recognize the potential of murals to tell stories and evoke emotions, these artful installations become indispensable tools for setting the mood in conference rooms.

Art as Icebreakers - Fostering Connection and Collaboration

Enter the realm of "Fostering Connection and Collaboration," the fourth chapter that explores how businesses are using art as icebreakers in meetings. Art has the unique ability to create common ground and serve as conversation starters. Consider a conference room with rotating art installations that change with each meeting, sparking discussions and encouraging participants to share their interpretations. Art as icebreakers goes beyond aesthetics; it becomes a catalyst for connection, opening avenues for collaboration and shared understanding.

The use of art as icebreakers recognizes that the dynamics of meetings are not solely about the agenda; they are also about the relationships and connections that form during discussions. By incorporating art that prompts dialogue and reflection, businesses create an environment where team members feel more at ease expressing their thoughts and ideas. As art becomes a bridge for communication, it fosters a culture of openness and collaboration within meetings.

Dynamic Installations - Engaging the Senses for Productive Discussions

"Dazzling Displays" unfolds as the fifth chapter, showcasing how businesses are engaging the senses with dynamic installations in conference rooms. Art is no longer confined to static pieces; businesses are incorporating dynamic installations that move, change colors, or respond to sound. Imagine a boardroom with interactive light installations that adjust based on the energy in the room or a brainstorming space with kinetic sculptures that move in sync with the flow of ideas. Dynamic installations engage the senses, creating an immersive environment that enhances focus and stimulates productive discussions.

The use of dynamic installations is a testament to the evolving role of art in meetings. Beyond being decorative, these installations actively contribute to the meeting experience by keeping participants visually engaged. As businesses experiment with the dynamic potential of art, they discover new ways to captivate attention, foster creativity, and make meetings more interactive and memorable.

Rotating Themes - Keeping Meetings Fresh and Inspiring

Conclude our exploration with "Keeping Meetings Fresh and Inspiring," the final chapter that emphasizes the value of rotating themes in conference rooms. Businesses recognize that the meeting environment plays a significant role in maintaining engagement and enthusiasm. Imagine a conference room that changes its theme monthly, featuring different artworks, colors, and arrangements to keep the space fresh and inspiring. Rotating themes ensure that the conference room remains an ever-evolving canvas that mirrors the dynamic nature of discussions and prevents monotony.

The beauty of rotating themes lies in their ability to surprise and stimulate creativity. When team members walk into a conference room with a new theme, it sparks curiosity and offers a refreshing perspective. As businesses embrace the concept of rotating themes, they ensure that the meeting environment remains a source of inspiration and motivation for ongoing discussions.

Window Wonders: A Masterclass in Drawing Foot Traffic with Artistic Retail Displays

The Artistry of Retail Windows

In the bustling world of retail, first impressions matter, and the artistry of retail windows plays a pivotal role in capturing the attention of passersby. In this blog post, we'll embark on a journey into the world of artistic retail displays, exploring how visually appealing windows can not only draw in foot traffic but also create a memorable and immersive shopping experience.

The Canvas of Curiosity - Crafting Compelling Window Displays

Retail windows are more than just glass panes; they're canvases waiting to tell a story. By actively curating displays that evoke curiosity, retailers can transform their storefronts into dynamic, ever-changing landscapes that captivate the attention of potential customers. Consider thematic displays that align with seasons, holidays, or special promotions, actively engaging with the pulse of the community.

Active participation in local events or collaborations with local artists can bring fresh and innovative perspectives to window displays. By actively curating displays that spark curiosity, retailers not only draw in foot traffic but also position their stores as dynamic and ever-evolving destinations.

Theatrical Allure - Creating Drama and Intrigue

Retail windows can be stages for theatrical displays that not only draw attention but create a sense of intrigue and excitement. Imagine passersby being drawn into a visual narrative that unfolds behind the glass. By actively incorporating elements of drama, movement, and unexpected surprises, retailers can transform their windows into mini-theatres that leave a lasting impression.

Active collaboration with visual merchandisers or artists who specialize in theatrical displays can elevate the impact of these window wonders. By actively infusing theatrical allure into retail displays, businesses not only draw in foot traffic but also create an immersive and memorable shopping experience that extends beyond the storefront.

Seasonal Symphony - Harmonizing with Holidays and Seasons

One of the most effective ways to draw foot traffic is by actively aligning window displays with seasons, holidays, and local events. From festive decorations during the holiday season to refreshing summer-themed displays, the active incorporation of seasonal elements creates an immediate connection with passersby. Imagine a clothing store with vibrant beach-themed displays in summer or a cozy bookstore adorned with autumnal hues in the fall.

Active planning and timely updates to align with seasons require a keen understanding of local trends and cultural nuances. By actively harmonizing window displays with the ebb and flow of seasons, retailers not only attract foot traffic but also create a sense of relevance and connection with the community.

Interactive Delights - Engaging with Passersby

In the age of experiential retail, the active incorporation of interactive elements into window displays can be a game-changer. Consider displays that invite passersby to touch, play, or participate in some way. From touchscreens displaying product information to interactive installations that respond to motion, the possibilities are endless. By actively engaging with the audience, retailers create a sense of involvement that extends from the sidewalk to the sales floor.

Active collaboration with tech-savvy artists or designers can bring a touch of innovation to interactive window displays. By actively incorporating interactive delights, retailers not only draw in foot traffic but also foster a sense of connection and excitement, turning window shopping into an engaging and participatory experience.

Local Flavor - Showcasing Community Connection

Retailers can actively draw in foot traffic by showcasing a strong connection to the local community through their window displays. Consider collaborations with local artists, featuring products from local vendors, or integrating elements that celebrate local landmarks and culture. This active participation in the community not only draws the attention of local residents but also positions the store as an integral part of the neighborhood.

Active involvement in community events, sponsorships, or partnerships with local organizations can contribute to the authenticity of the displays. By actively showcasing local flavor in window displays, retailers not only draw in foot traffic but also build a loyal customer base that appreciates the store's commitment to community connection.

Ever-Evolving Artistry - Keeping Displays Fresh and Relevant

The art of drawing foot traffic through retail windows is an ever-evolving journey. Regular updates and fresh perspectives are essential to maintaining relevance and visual appeal. Actively plan for rotations, seasonal changes, or themed displays to ensure that the storefront remains a dynamic and inviting space for passersby. Consider engaging with feedback from customers or monitoring trends to stay ahead of the curve.

Active collaboration with visual merchandisers, local artists, or even in-house creative teams can contribute to the constant evolution of window displays. By actively embracing the artistry of change, retailers not only draw in foot traffic consistently but also create a sense of anticipation, turning window shopping into a delightful and ever-renewing experience.

Turning Windows into Welcoming Portals

In the world of retail, the artistry of window displays goes beyond aesthetics; it's about creating welcoming portals that draw in foot traffic and set the stage for memorable shopping experiences. By actively infusing creativity, theatrical allure, and community connection into retail windows, businesses can transform passersby into engaged customers, making the storefront a destination in itself.

Bringing Nature Indoors: Greening Up Commercial Spaces with Botanical Art

Step into the lush world of "Bringing Nature Indoors," where we explore the enchanting realm of botanical art and its transformative impact on commercial spaces. In this verdant journey, discover how the integration of botanical elements within business environments not only brings a breath of fresh air but also fosters a harmonious and revitalizing ambiance.

The Botanical Renaissance: Embracing Nature's Aesthetic

In "The Botanical Renaissance," we embark on a journey through the resurgence of botanical art in commercial spaces. Explore how businesses are increasingly turning to botanical themes to create visually stunning and biophilic interiors. Dive into the aesthetic appeal of vibrant greenery, intricate foliage, and the diverse world of plant-inspired art, bringing a touch of the outdoors inside.

Consider incorporating botanical murals, prints, and installations that echo the beauty of nature, transforming your commercial space into a serene oasis.

Biophilia in Business: Nurturing Employee Well-being

In "Biophilia in Business," discover the science behind biophilic design and its positive impact on employee well-being. Delve into how botanical art fosters a connection with nature, reduces stress, and enhances productivity. Explore case studies showcasing businesses that have embraced biophilic principles, creating work environments that prioritize the health and happiness of their employees.

Consider introducing potted plants, vertical gardens, and botanical-themed workspaces to infuse natural elements into your business environment.

The Power of Green: Sustainable and Eco-Friendly Art Choices

"The Power of Green" explores the sustainability aspect of botanical art choices for commercial spaces. Uncover how businesses can align with eco-friendly practices by selecting artwork that reflects a commitment to the environment. Learn about artists using sustainable materials and techniques, contributing to a green and responsible approach to decorating business interiors.

Consider collaborating with artists or art vendors who prioritize sustainable practices, ensuring your botanical art choices are environmentally conscious.

Beyond Paintings: Innovations in Botanical Art Installations

In "Beyond Paintings," we push the boundaries of traditional botanical art by exploring innovative installations. From living walls to suspended gardens, discover how businesses are embracing three-dimensional botanical art to create immersive and captivating environments. Explore the versatility of botanical art installations in transforming commercial spaces into unique and memorable settings.

Consider commissioning custom botanical installations that

complement the architecture and layout of your business space, providing a captivating visual experience.

Botanical Branding: Infusing Company Identity with Nature's Palette

"Botanical Branding" delves into the concept of using botanical elements to infuse company identity with nature's palette. Explore how businesses can integrate botanical art that aligns with their brand colors, values, and messaging. Learn about the psychological impact of specific plant motifs and how they can contribute to a positive and memorable brand image.

Consider incorporating botanical patterns, motifs, or logos inspired by nature into your branding elements, creating a cohesive and visually appealing identity.

Curating a Green Gallery: Showcasing Botanical Diversity

In "Curating a Green Gallery," we explore the art of curating a collection that celebrates the diversity of botanical art. Discover how businesses can showcase a variety of plant-inspired pieces, from classic floral paintings to contemporary botanical photography. Learn about the role of curation in creating a visually engaging and harmonious gallery that resonates with employees and visitors alike.

Consider hosting gallery events or rotating exhibits to keep your botanical art collection dynamic and reflective of the ever-changing seasons.

To Wrap Up:

In "Bringing Nature Indoors: Greening Up Commercial Spaces with Botanical Art," we've uncovered the myriad ways in which businesses can benefit from the infusion of botanical elements into their interiors. From promoting well-being to embracing sustainability, botanical art provides a versatile and aesthetically pleasing solution for businesses seeking to create vibrant, nature-inspired environments. Elevate your commercial space into a green oasis that not only captivates but rejuvenates.

Networking in Colors: Mastering the Art of Business-Oriented Art Installation

The Canvas of Connection

Welcome to the vibrant world of Networking in Colors, where the art of networking converges with the world of captivating installations. In this blog post, we unravel the strategic dance between business and art, exploring how creative installations can transform spaces into networking havens. From corporate galleries to interactive exhibits, discover the artful inspirations that are reshaping the dynamics of professional connections.

The Power of First Impressions - Crafting Entrances That Spark Conversations

Begin our journey with "Crafting Entrances That Spark Conversations," the first chapter that unveils how businesses are using art to make impactful first impressions. The entrance to a networking event sets the stage for connections, and businesses are leveraging art to create immersive experiences. Picture a corporate lobby adorned with dynamic sculptures or an entrance pathway featuring interactive light installations. Crafting entrances that spark conversations not only captivates attendees but also sets a positive tone, breaking the ice and encouraging meaningful interactions from the start.

The power of these artistic entrances lies in their ability to create a welcoming and memorable atmosphere. When attendees walk into a networking event and are greeted by thoughtfully curated art, it fosters a sense of excitement and engagement. Businesses recognize that the first impression goes beyond handshakes; it's an artful dance that begins with the visual allure of the environment, establishing a foundation for successful networking.

Thematic Networking Lounges - Transforming Spaces Into Conversation Hubs

Dive into the second chapter, "Transforming Spaces Into Conversation Hubs," where we explore how businesses are creating thematic networking lounges that elevate the art of conversation. Networking isn't confined to formal settings; it thrives in spaces designed for connection. Imagine an event with themed lounges, each adorned with art installations that align with specific industries or topics. Thematic networking lounges not only provide a relaxed atmosphere for interactions but also serve as visual cues that guide attendees towards like-minded individuals, fostering more meaningful and targeted networking.

The transformative impact of thematic networking lounges lies in their ability to cater to diverse interests and industries. When attendees can gravitate towards spaces that resonate with their professional focus, it streamlines networking efforts and creates a more efficient and enjoyable experience. Businesses are recognizing that these thematic havens add layers of depth to networking events, turning them into immersive journeys where connections are not just made but curated.

Corporate Galleries - Merging Business and Art for Lasting Impressions

"Canvas Conversations: Merging Business and Art" unfolds as the third chapter, showcasing how businesses are curating corporate galleries that become the focal points of networking events. Galleries are no longer reserved for traditional art; they are becoming dynamic spaces where business and creativity converge. Imagine an event with a dedicated gallery space featuring artworks that mirror the values and achievements of the attending companies. Corporate galleries not only celebrate the businesses present but also serve as conversation starters, creating an environment where networking becomes a visual and intellectual exploration.

The transformative impact of corporate galleries lies in their ability to leave lasting impressions on attendees. When businesses showcase their achievements and aspirations through carefully selected artworks, it creates a sense of pride and connection. Attendees find themselves not only exchanging business cards but also engaging in conversations sparked by the visual narratives within the gallery. Businesses recognize that these curated spaces elevate the networking experience, making it more memorable and meaningful.

Interactive Exhibits - Catalyzing Connections Through Participation

Enter the realm of "Participation Stations," the fourth chapter that explores how businesses are catalyzing connections through interactive exhibits. Networking is an active endeavor, and businesses are transforming static displays into dynamic participation stations. Picture an event with interactive art installations that encourage attendees to contribute their thoughts, ideas, or even collaborate on a live artwork. Participation stations not only engage the senses but also turn networking into a hands-on and memorable experience.

The transformative impact of participation stations lies in their ability to break down barriers and facilitate organic conversations. When attendees actively participate in creating or interacting with art, it creates shared experiences that become the foundation for lasting connections. Businesses are recognizing that these interactive exhibits add an element of playfulness to networking events, fostering a culture of engagement and collaboration.

Networking Walls - Showcasing Attendees and Facilitating Connections

"Dazzling Databases: Networking Walls" unfolds as the fifth chapter, showcasing how businesses are using networking walls to showcase attendees and facilitate connections. Networking isn't just about meeting new people; it's also about recognizing the diverse talents and expertise present in the room. Imagine an event with a digital networking wall displaying attendee profiles, achievements, and areas of expertise. Networking walls not only provide a visual directory but also serve as powerful tools for connecting individuals with shared interests and goals.

The transformative impact of networking walls lies in their ability to democratize networking and create a sense of community. When attendees can easily identify potential connections based on shared interests or complementary skills, it streamlines the networking process. Businesses recognize that these digital canvases go beyond traditional name tags, adding a layer of sophistication to networking events and fostering a culture of collaboration and mutual support.

Networking Through Artful Experiences - Creating Memories That Endure

Conclude our exploration with "Creating Memories That Endure," the final chapter that emphasizes the value of artful experiences in networking. Networking isn't just about exchanging business cards; it's about creating lasting memories. Imagine an event with live art performances, collaborative mural creations, or art-themed activities that become the shared experiences attendees carry with them. Artful experiences not only enhance the networking event but also ensure that the connections made are memorable and enduring.

The beauty of artful experiences lies in their ability to transcend the boundaries of traditional networking. When attendees can bond over shared creative activities, it creates a sense of camaraderie that extends beyond the event. Businesses recognize that these artful experiences contribute to a positive and lasting impression, making networking events not just productive but also enjoyable and enriching.

Creative Havens: Unleashing Inspiration in Art Studios with Wall Decor Ideas

Welcome to the world of boundless inspiration and artistic expression! In this blog post, we'll explore the enchanting realm of art studios and delve into the transformative power of wall decor. Whether you're a seasoned artist or just starting, join us on a journey through the six creative sections that will turn your art studio into a haven of inspiration and innovation.

The Canvas of Creativity: Choosing the Perfect Studio Colors

In "The Canvas of Creativity," we begin by discussing the importance of choosing the perfect colors for your art studio. Dive into the psychology of colors and how they impact creativity. From soothing blues to energizing yellows, discover how the right color palette can set the tone for your studio space.

Consider opting for neutral tones as a backdrop to allow your artwork to take center stage. The canvas of creativity is all about creating a harmonious and inspiring environment that encourages artistic expression.

Gallery Wall Wonders: Showcasing Your Artistic Journey

In "Gallery Wall Wonders," we explore the magic of showcasing your artistic journey through a carefully curated gallery wall. Learn how to arrange your artwork to tell a visual story, from early sketches to finished masterpieces. Discover the joy of surrounding yourself with your own creations as a constant source of inspiration.

Consider incorporating a mix of framed paintings, sketches, and even snippets of your creative process on a dedicated gallery wall. Gallery wall wonders transform your studio into a dynamic and evolving space that reflects the evolution of your artistic endeavors.

Organizing Chaos: Functional and Stylish Studio Storage

"Organizing Chaos" delves into the crucial aspect of studio storage. Explore functional and stylish storage solutions that keep your art supplies in order without sacrificing aesthetic appeal. From open shelving to colorful storage bins, find the balance between accessibility and visual appeal.

Consider repurposing vintage furniture or installing custom shelving units to create a personalized storage system. Organizing chaos ensures that your studio remains an inviting and clutter-free space, allowing your creativity to flow without hindrance.

Artistic Illumination: Shedding Light on Creativity

In "Artistic Illumination," we shed light on the transformative power of lighting in an art studio. Explore the role of natural light, task lighting, and ambient illumination in creating a well-lit and visually engaging workspace. Learn how to optimize lighting to enhance your focus and productivity.

Consider installing adjustable task lights for detailed work areas and maximizing natural light sources wherever possible. Artistic illumination ensures that your studio is bathed in the perfect glow, providing an inviting atmosphere for your artistic pursuits.

The Statement Easel: Elevating Your Creative Centerpiece

"The Statement Easel" takes center stage as we explore the impact of this essential tool in your art studio. Discover how the right easel can become a statement piece that not only supports your creative process but also adds a touch of elegance to your space. From traditional wooden easels to modern, adjustable options, find the perfect centerpiece for your studio.

Consider choosing an easel that complements your studio's aesthetic, whether it's a classic tripod design or a sleek, contemporary option. The statement easel transforms your creative corner into a focal point that inspires your artistic endeavors.

Personalized Inspirations: Adding a Touch of You

In the final section, "Personalized Inspirations," we explore the art of adding personal touches to your studio decor. From sentimental objects to custom-made art prints, discover how infusing your personality into your studio space creates an environment that truly feels like your own.

Consider incorporating elements that hold special meaning to you, such as family photos, personal mementos, or artworks from fellow artists. Personalized inspirations ensure that your studio becomes a reflection of your identity, making it a space where creativity flourishes effortlessly.

Conclusion:

As we conclude our exploration of art studios and wall decor ideas, remember that the true essence of a creative haven lies in the unique fusion of functionality and personal expression. Whether you're choosing the perfect studio colors, creating gallery wall wonders, organizing chaos with stylish storage, optimizing artistic illumination, elevating your creative centerpiece with a statement easel, or adding personalized inspirations, each section unveils a facet of the transformative power that wall decor holds in cultivating a space where inspiration knows no bounds.

Pixels and Progress: Elevating Gaming and Tech Spaces with Futuristic Art for Innovators

The Canvas of the Future in Gaming and Tech Spaces

Embark on a journey into the future where pixels meet progress, and tech spaces become canvases for futuristic artistry. In this blog post, we'll explore the dynamic intersection of gaming and technology with forward-thinking businesses that leverage futuristic art to create immersive environments. From cutting-edge installations to digital masterpieces, discover how the art of the future is transforming gaming and tech spaces.

Pixels in Harmony - The Artful Integration of Technology

Pixels in Harmony sets the stage for our exploration, highlighting the artful integration of technology into gaming and tech spaces. Modern businesses recognize the importance of blending art seamlessly with technology to create immersive and visually stunning environments. Consider LED walls that respond to user interactions, creating a dynamic visual experience. Embrace digital canvases that showcase futuristic animations, transforming spaces into interactive realms where art and technology coalesce.

The artful integration of pixels not only enhances the aesthetic appeal but also contributes to the overall user experience. Imagine a gaming lounge where walls come alive with vibrant pixel art, reacting to the energy of the players. By harmonizing pixels and technology, businesses cultivate environments that captivate, inspire, and push the boundaries of what's possible in gaming and tech spaces.

VR Vistas - Navigating Virtual Worlds Through Art

VR Vistas unfolds as a chapter dedicated to navigating virtual worlds through art, transforming gaming and tech spaces into gateways to unexplored realms. Virtual Reality (VR) spaces are not just about cutting-edge technology; they are also opportunities for artistic expression. Consider VR installations that transport users to visually stunning landscapes or immersive digital galleries. These spaces become canvases for artists to craft experiences that transcend physical limitations, offering users a journey through the extraordinary.

Collaborate with digital artists to create VR environments that not only showcase their talents but also push the boundaries of what is conceivable in the virtual realm. VR Vistas redefine the concept of art spaces by allowing users to step into the artwork itself, blurring the lines between the physical and the digital. In this futuristic landscape, gaming and tech spaces become portals to endless possibilities where users can explore, interact, and be enveloped by art in unprecedented ways.

Augmented Realms - Enhancing Reality Through Art

Augmented Realms emerge as a captivating dimension where reality is enhanced through art, revolutionizing the way we perceive gaming and tech spaces. Augmented Reality (AR) technologies bring digital elements into the physical world, allowing businesses to overlay futuristic art onto real-world environments. Imagine a tech showroom where products come to life through AR animations or a gaming arena where players interact with augmented elements seamlessly integrated into the space.

The enhancement of reality through art not only provides an engaging experience for users but also serves as a tool for storytelling and brand expression. Businesses can leverage AR to create interactive exhibits, where users can unlock hidden art elements by exploring the space with their devices. Augmented Realms redefine the spatial experience, turning gaming and tech spaces into dynamic environments that transcend the traditional boundaries of art and reality.

Neon Horizons - Illuminating Spaces with Futuristic Illumination

Neon Horizons light up the narrative, showcasing the transformative power of futuristic illumination in gaming and tech spaces. Neon lights have long been associated with futurism, and businesses are embracing this aesthetic to elevate their spaces. Consider neon installations that outline the contours of gaming stations, futuristic sculptures that emit ethereal glows, or immersive LED ceilings that mimic the night sky. Neon Horizons bring an otherworldly ambiance to gaming and tech spaces, creating an atmosphere that feels straight out of a cyberpunk dream.

The use of neon and futuristic illumination not only adds a visual spectacle but also reinforces the theme of innovation and progress. These vibrant lights turn gaming lounges into dynamic landscapes, and tech offices into energized hubs of creativity. Neon Horizons transform spaces into futuristic realms where the interplay of light and art becomes an integral part of the user experience.

Interactive Installations - Bridging Play and Art

Interactive Installations bridge the gap between play and art, creating dynamic spaces that respond to user engagement. Businesses are incorporating installations that invite users to interact physically with the art, blurring the lines between observer and participant. Consider touch-sensitive walls that react to gestures, interactive floors that respond to movement, or even collaborative installations where multiple users can contribute to a digital masterpiece. These installations redefine the relationship between users and art, transforming gaming and tech spaces into dynamic playgrounds of creativity.

The integration of interactive elements not only enhances user engagement but also fosters a sense of ownership and connection. Users become active participants in the artistic experience, influencing and shaping the evolving artwork in real-time. Interactive Installations turn gaming and tech spaces into arenas of co-creation, where users are not just consumers of art but collaborators in the artistic process.

Futuristic Expression - Crafting Identity in Gaming and Tech Spaces

As the final stroke on the canvas of futuristic art in gaming and tech spaces, Futuristic Expression becomes the theme that defines the identity of these innovative environments. Businesses are actively crafting their identities through artistic expressions that align with their brand narratives. Consider custom installations that reflect the ethos of a tech company, or gaming spaces adorned with futuristic murals that resonate with the gaming community. Futuristic Expression goes beyond mere decoration; it becomes a powerful tool for businesses to communicate their values, aspirations, and commitment to pushing the boundaries of technology and creativity.

Futuristic Expression not only defines the aesthetic character of gaming and tech spaces but also serves as a beacon that attracts like-minded individuals. Businesses become pioneers in crafting unique and identifiable spaces that resonate with the futuristic visions of their users. As gaming and tech spaces evolve, Futuristic Expression ensures that these environments not only keep up with the times but actively shape the narrative of the future.

Canvas Collaboration: Crafting Open Office Harmony Through Art

The Art of Balance in Open Offices

In the dynamic world of open offices, where collaboration is key, finding the right balance between interaction and focus can be a challenge. Enter the transformative power of art. This blog post explores how strategically incorporating art into open office spaces can define zones, foster creativity, and create a harmonious work environment that strikes the perfect balance between collaboration and concentration.

The Entrance Statement - Setting the Tone with Welcome Walls

First impressions matter, and the entrance of your open office sets the tone for the entire space. Consider creating a visually striking entrance statement using art that reflects your company culture and values. Bold murals, dynamic sculptures, or even a thought-provoking gallery wall can instantly communicate the personality of your workplace. This not only makes the entrance visually appealing but also serves as a subtle guide for employees and visitors, signaling the transition into the collaborative realm beyond.

The entrance statement doesn't just stop at aesthetics; it contributes to a sense of identity and belonging. When employees and visitors are greeted by a carefully curated art display, it creates a shared visual language that connects everyone in the space. It's a welcoming gesture that fosters a positive atmosphere and sets the stage for open office harmony.

Artful Zones - Defining Spaces for Focus and Collaboration

Open offices thrive on collaboration, but they also require areas for focused work. Use art to visually define different zones within the space. For collaborative areas, consider vibrant and energizing art that sparks creativity. This could be colorful murals, interactive installations, or even a rotating display of employee artwork. These zones become dynamic hubs where ideas flow freely, and the atmosphere is conducive to brainstorming and teamwork.

In contrast, designate quieter areas for focused work or individual tasks. Use calming colors, subtle artwork, or even acoustic panels adorned with art to create a serene environment. The strategic use of art helps employees intuitively understand the purpose of each space, promoting a harmonious flow between collaboration and concentration within the open office.

The Power of Personalization - Employee-Curated Workspaces

Empower employees to personalize their workspaces with art that inspires them. Instead of uniformity, embrace diversity in individual workspaces. Allow employees to bring in their favorite artwork, whether it's paintings, prints, or even personal creations. This not only adds a touch of personality to the open office but also fosters a sense of ownership and well-being among employees.

Encourage art swaps or rotating displays to keep the environment fresh and dynamic. Personalized workspaces contribute to a positive company culture, where employees feel valued and engaged. The walls of an open office become a collective gallery of individual expressions, creating an environment that celebrates diversity and creativity while still maintaining a cohesive overall aesthetic.

Navigational Art - Wayfinding in Open Office Labyrinths

The vastness of open offices can sometimes make navigation a challenge. Use art as a functional and aesthetic solution for wayfinding. Install thematic art or unique installations in strategic locations to serve as visual landmarks. This not only aids in navigation but also transforms the journey through the office into an engaging experience.

Consider using different art styles or color schemes for each section of the office to create a visual map. For example, a section with blue hues might signify meeting areas, while a section with warm tones could indicate collaborative spaces. Navigational art not only adds practical value but also turns the act of moving through the open office into a curated experience, enhancing the overall ambiance.

Seasonal Surprises - Temporal Transformations Through Art

Keep the open office environment dynamic and fresh by introducing seasonal art installations. Themed artwork can transform the atmosphere and bring a sense of novelty to the space. Whether it's springtime florals, summer-inspired colors, or cozy fall motifs, seasonal art installations inject a vibrant energy that resonates with the changing seasons.

These temporal transformations don't have to be grand; even small changes, like rotating art prints or introducing seasonal decor, can make a significant impact. It not only keeps the office visually interesting but also contributes to a positive and adaptable workplace culture, where change is embraced and celebrated.

Artistic Reflections - Fostering Well-Being and Creativity

Art has the power to influence mood and well-being. Use reflective and calming artwork strategically placed near break areas or lounges to create spaces for relaxation and rejuvenation. Incorporate elements like nature-inspired art, soft color palettes, or even tranquil sounds to promote a sense of calm. These areas become retreats within the open office, allowing employees to recharge and return to their tasks with renewed focus.

Additionally, consider dedicating spaces for creative expression. Install writable walls or chalkboard surfaces where employees can doodle, jot down ideas, or collaborate visually. The freedom to express ideas in a non-conventional way fosters creativity and contributes to a culture of innovation within the open office environment.

Conclusion: Masterpiece in Motion - Crafting Open Office Harmony

In the canvas of open offices, art isn't just decoration; it's a tool for crafting harmony. From defining zones to fostering creativity, strategically incorporating art transforms the workplace into a masterpiece in motion. By recognizing the influence of art on the work environment, companies can create open offices that balance collaboration and concentration, reflecting a positive company culture and elevating the overall employee experience.

Industrial Chic: Artistic Elements for Warehouse and Industrial Spaces

Welcome to the world of "Industrial Chic," where gritty aesthetics meet artistic expression in warehouse and industrial spaces. In this blog post, we'll explore how the marriage of raw industrial elements and curated art can transform these spaces into dynamic, inspiring environments that seamlessly blend rugged charm with creative flair.

The Canvas of Concrete: Embracing Industrial Backdrops

In "The Canvas of Concrete," we delve into the unique appeal of concrete as a backdrop for artistic expression. Explore how the rough texture and neutral tones of concrete walls provide an ideal canvas for a variety of art styles, from large-scale murals to minimalist installations. Discover the beauty of juxtaposing the industrial with the artistic to create a visually striking and harmonious environment.

Consider commissioning local street artists to create murals that celebrate the industrial history of the space while injecting a burst of color and creativity.

Metallic Marvels: Elevating Spaces with Industrial Art Installations

In "Metallic Marvels," we shine a spotlight on the versatility of metal as a medium for industrial art installations. From welded sculptures to abstract metal compositions, learn how artists are repurposing industrial materials to create eye-catching pieces that complement the robust nature of warehouse spaces. Dive into the world of metalworkers and sculptors who bring an edgy elegance to industrial settings.

Consider incorporating custom metal art installations that reflect the functional aspects of the space while adding a touch of artistic sophistication.

Repurposed Relics: Giving New Life to Industrial Salvage

In "Repurposed Relics," we explore the trend of repurposing industrial salvage into unique art pieces. From reclaimed wood to discarded machinery parts, discover how artists and designers are breathing new life into forgotten relics, turning them into conversation-starting art installations. Learn about the sustainability aspect of using salvaged materials in art, contributing to the overall eco-friendly ethos of the space.

Consider collaborating with local artisans who specialize in repurposing industrial artifacts to create bespoke art pieces that tell a story of the space's history.

Walls of Wires: Sculptural Art in Industrial Wire Mesh

In "Walls of Wires," we unravel the artistic potential of industrial wire mesh in creating sculptural art pieces. Explore how artists are manipulating wire mesh to form intricate and three-dimensional artworks that add depth and character to industrial spaces. Learn about the play of light and shadow on wire mesh sculptures, creating a dynamic visual experience.

Consider integrating wire mesh sculptures strategically within the space to delineate different areas or to serve as unique focal points.

Functional Art: The Fusion of Aesthetics and Utility in Industrial Spaces

In "Functional Art," we explore the innovative concept of merging aesthetics with utility in industrial spaces. Discover how artists and designers are creating functional art pieces that serve a dual purpose – enhancing the visual appeal of the space while fulfilling practical needs. From industrial-style furniture to art-inspired lighting fixtures, learn about the seamless integration of form and function.

Consider investing in custom-made furniture or lighting fixtures that align with the industrial theme, elevating the overall design and functionality of the space.

Interactive Experiences: Artistic Installations for Employee Engagement

In "Interactive Experiences," we highlight the power of artistic installations in fostering employee engagement and well-being. Explore how interactive art installations, such as wall-mounted kinetic sculptures or collaborative mural projects, create a sense of ownership and community among employees. Learn about the positive impact of incorporating art that invites participation and encourages a collaborative spirit.

Consider organizing team-building activities around the creation of interactive art installations, promoting a sense of camaraderie and shared creativity.

In Conclusion:

In "Industrial Chic: Artistic Elements for Warehouse and Industrial Spaces," we've uncovered the myriad ways in which art can seamlessly integrate with the raw charm of industrial environments. By embracing the concept of industrial chic, these spaces can become not just functional but also visually captivating, inspiring creativity and fostering a unique identity.

Curating a Gallery: Showcasing Local Artists in Business Spaces

In the captivating world of "Curating a Gallery," we explore the transformative impact of incorporating local art into business spaces. This blog post takes you on a journey through the synergy of commerce and creativity, highlighting the benefits of curating galleries within corporate environments. From fostering a vibrant work culture to supporting local artists, discover how businesses can turn their spaces into galleries that inspire and engage.

Beyond White Walls: Rethinking Corporate Spaces

In "Beyond White Walls," we challenge the conventional aesthetics of corporate spaces. Explore how businesses can break free from the monotony of white walls by infusing vibrant, local artwork into their environments. Learn about the positive impact this has on employee morale, productivity, and the overall atmosphere of the workspace. Discover how an art-infused workplace can become a source of inspiration and creativity.

Consider incorporating bold, eye-catching pieces that reflect the company's values and culture, transforming your workspace into a dynamic gallery.

Fostering Local Talent: Building Community Connections

"Fostering Local Talent" dives into the enriching experience of supporting and showcasing artists from the local community. Discover the importance of building connections with local artists and how businesses can contribute to the flourishing arts scene. Learn about the mutually beneficial relationships that can be forged, creating a sense of community and shared success between businesses and artists.

Consider establishing partnerships with local art organizations or hosting events to discover and support emerging talent within your community.

Art for Employee Well-being: Nurturing a Creative Work Environment

In "Art for Employee Well-being," explore the significant impact of art on employee well-being. Uncover how curated galleries in business spaces contribute to a positive and stress-free work environment. Delve into the psychology of colors, forms, and artistic expressions, understanding how these elements can enhance the mental health and overall happiness of employees.

Consider conducting art workshops or providing designated spaces for employees to showcase their own artistic talents, fostering a sense of creative expression within the workplace.

Corporate Collections: Investing in Cultural Capital

"Corporate Collections" delves into the concept of businesses investing in cultural capital through art. Explore how curated galleries can become a unique selling point for businesses, attracting clients and customers who appreciate a visually stimulating environment. Learn about the long-term value of creating a corporate art collection and how it can contribute to the overall brand image of the company.

Consider collaborating with art curators or consultants to create a curated collection that aligns with the values and identity of your business.

Art as a Storytelling Medium: Communicating Company Values

In "Art as a Storytelling Medium," we explore how businesses can use art to communicate their values and narratives. Discover the power of visual storytelling and how curated galleries can serve as a medium to convey the ethos, mission, and vision of a company. Learn about the various ways businesses can align their brand narrative with the art they choose to display.

Consider hosting curated gallery events that narrate the story of your company, creating an immersive experience for clients, employees, and visitors.

The Curator's Role: Navigating the Artistic Landscape

In "The Curator's Role," we shed light on the pivotal role of a curator in shaping the artistic landscape of business spaces. Explore the expertise needed to curate a gallery that harmonizes with the company's culture, values, and aesthetic preferences. Learn about the delicate balance between showcasing diverse artistic styles while maintaining a cohesive and engaging gallery environment.

Consider hiring a professional curator or forming an internal committee to ensure the curation process aligns with the company's vision and goals.

Conclusion:

In "Curating a Gallery: Showcasing Local Artists in Business Spaces," we've uncovered the myriad ways in which businesses can benefit from incorporating local art into their environments. From fostering community connections to enhancing employee well-being, the curated gallery serves as a bridge between commerce and culture. Elevate your business space into a living gallery that not only showcases local talent but also communicates the unique story and values of your company.

Creating a Welcoming Atmosphere: The Impact of Wall Art in Reception Areas

Step into the world of first impressions with "Creating a Welcoming Atmosphere: The Impact of Wall Art in Reception Areas." In this blog post, we explore the artistry behind crafting inviting reception spaces and how the right wall art can transform these areas into warm and engaging environments. From color psychology to design elements, discover the secrets to making your reception area a visual delight for guests and visitors.

The Art of First Impressions: Designing Welcoming Reception Areas

In "The Art of First Impressions," we unravel the importance of crafting reception areas that leave a lasting impact. Explore the psychology behind first impressions and learn how thoughtful design choices, including wall art selection, can set the tone for a positive and welcoming experience. Dive into case studies of businesses that have successfully curated reception spaces, creating an environment that resonates with their brand identity and values.

Consider incorporating elements like vibrant artwork, comfortable seating, and strategic lighting to create a welcoming ambiance that reflects your company's personality.

Beyond Aesthetics: The Functional Role of Art in Reception Areas

Discover "Beyond Aesthetics" as we delve into the functional role of art in reception areas. Explore how artwork can serve as more than just decoration, acting as wayfinding tools, brand storytellers, and even functional installations. Learn from examples of businesses that have seamlessly integrated art into their reception areas to enhance functionality and improve the overall guest experience.

Consider incorporating interactive elements, such as digital displays or rotating art exhibits, to keep the reception area dynamic and engaging for visitors.

Branding Brilliance: Using Wall Art to Reinforce Corporate Identity

In "Branding Brilliance," we explore how wall art can be a powerful tool for reinforcing corporate identity in reception areas. Understand the impact of cohesive branding through color schemes, logo placement, and thematic art choices. Delve into the world of businesses that have effectively utilized wall art to create a visual narrative that aligns with their brand message.

Consider commissioning custom art pieces that incorporate your brand colors and values, turning your reception area into a visual representation of your corporate identity.

Cultural Connections: Celebrating Diversity Through Art in Reception Spaces

In "Cultural Connections," we highlight the importance of celebrating diversity in reception areas through art. Explore how businesses can create inclusive and culturally rich environments by featuring artwork that represents a variety of perspectives. Learn from companies that have successfully integrated diverse art collections into their reception spaces, fostering a sense of belonging for all visitors.

Consider partnering with local artists or organizations to feature culturally diverse artwork, creating a reception area that reflects the global nature of your business.

Spatial Harmony: Balancing Art with Reception Area Layouts

In "Spatial Harmony," we delve into the art of balancing wall art with reception area layouts. Explore the impact of spatial design on the overall aesthetic and functionality of the space. Learn how to create a harmonious visual flow that guides guests seamlessly through the reception area while maximizing the potential of wall art to enhance the spatial experience.

Consider experimenting with different layouts, wall arrangements, and lighting techniques to achieve a balanced and visually appealing reception area.

Dynamic Displays: Rotating Art to Keep Reception Areas Fresh

In our final section, "Dynamic Displays," we explore the concept of rotating art to keep reception areas fresh and dynamic. Understand the benefits of regularly updating artwork to reflect seasonal themes, special occasions, or evolving brand narratives. Dive into case studies of businesses that have successfully implemented rotating art displays, keeping their reception areas vibrant and engaging.

Consider establishing a schedule for art rotations, incorporating both permanent and temporary pieces to keep the reception area visually stimulating and ever-evolving.

Conclusion:

In "Creating a Welcoming Atmosphere: The Impact of

Wall Art in Reception Areas," we've unraveled the secrets to transforming reception spaces into welcoming havens. Elevate your first point of contact with visitors, leaving a lasting impression through thoughtful design, functional art choices, and a celebration of diversity. Craft a reception area that not only reflects your brand identity but also sets the stage for positive interactions and memorable experiences.

Artful Bites: The Fusion of Flavor and Form in Restaurant Design

The Gastronomic Canvas - Art and Ambiance in Dining Spaces

Welcome to the delectable world of "Artful Bites," where the culinary experience extends beyond the plate to embrace the entire restaurant ambiance. In this blog post, we'll explore the marriage of flavor and form, uncovering how restaurants are integrating art into their design to create immersive and unforgettable dining spaces. From avant-garde murals to interactive table settings, discover how culinary creativity and artistic expression converge to elevate the dining experience.

The Art of Appetite - Setting the Stage for Culinary Exploration

Our journey begins with "Setting the Stage for Culinary Exploration," where we delve into how restaurants are using art to craft a visual prelude to the gastronomic journey. Imagine entering a restaurant with walls adorned in vibrant murals depicting the ingredients of the chef's signature dishes or a cozy café with artistic installations that mirror the spirit of the local community. Setting the stage for culinary exploration not only stimulates the appetite but also establishes a unique identity for the restaurant, making it a destination where patrons embark on a multisensory adventure.

The transformative power of this artistic prelude lies in its ability to cultivate a sense of anticipation and excitement. When patrons step into a restaurant greeted by visually engaging elements, it elevates the entire dining experience, making it more than a meal—it becomes an immersive journey. Restaurants recognize that this intentional fusion of art and ambiance not only entices diners but also sets the tone for the culinary delights that await.

Murals on the Menu - Culinary Narratives Unleashed on Walls

Dive into the second chapter, "Culinary Narratives Unleashed on Walls," where we explore how restaurants are using murals as storytelling mediums that transcend the confines of the menu. Murals go beyond being decorative; they become visual feasts that narrate the culinary journey of the establishment. Picture a seafood restaurant with a mural showcasing the ocean's bounty or a farm-to-table eatery with a wall painting illustrating the journey from farm to plate. Culinary narratives unleashed on walls not only provide aesthetic appeal but also immerse diners in the narrative behind the dishes, creating a more intimate and engaging dining experience.

The transformative impact of these murals lies in their ability to forge a deeper connection between diners and the culinary offerings. When patrons can visually absorb the stories behind the menu, it adds a layer of appreciation and understanding to their dining experience. Restaurants recognize that these murals serve as culinary ambassadors, inviting diners to embark on a gastronomic journey that extends far beyond the confines of the plate.

Interactive Dining Experiences - Taste

and Touch Merge in Artful Settings

"Elevating Dining through Interactive Experiences" unfolds as the third chapter, showcasing how restaurants are incorporating interactive elements that invite patrons to engage with art while savoring their meals. Imagine a sushi restaurant with interactive table projections that display information about the origin of the fish or a dessert bar where diners can create edible art on touch-sensitive tables. Elevating dining through interactive experiences not only stimulates the senses but also transforms the act of eating into a participatory and memorable event.

The transformative power of interactive dining experiences lies in their ability to turn a meal into a dynamic and immersive occasion. When diners can actively engage with art while enjoying their food, it adds an element of playfulness and novelty to the dining experience. Restaurants recognize that these interactive elements not only differentiate them in a competitive culinary landscape but also contribute to creating lasting memories for their patrons.

Sculptural Gastronomy - Artistic Elements Beyond the Plate

Enter the realm of "Sculptural Gastronomy," the fourth chapter that explores how restaurants are incorporating three-dimensional art into their design, extending beyond traditional paintings or murals. Sculptures and installations become integral elements, creating a dynamic and visually stunning environment. Picture a modern fusion restaurant with suspended sculptures inspired by the fusion of cultures or a wine bar with cascading artistic elements representing the aging process of wine. Sculptural gastronomy not only adds aesthetic value but also transforms the dining space into an immersive and thought-provoking environment.

The transformative impact of sculptural gastronomy lies in its ability to blur the lines between art and cuisine. When patrons encounter three-dimensional art within the dining space, it creates a sense of wonder and curiosity, enhancing the overall dining experience. Restaurants recognize that these sculptural elements contribute to the uniqueness of the venue, making it a destination not just for exceptional cuisine but also for artistic exploration.

Cultural Fusion on the Plate and Palette - Designing Culinary Experiences

"Cultural Fusion on the Plate and Palette" unfolds as the fifth chapter, showcasing how restaurants are designing culinary experiences that harmonize with the cultural elements reflected in their artistic decor. Picture a Mexican restaurant with vibrant murals depicting traditional celebrations and a menu that echoes the rich flavors of the region. Cultural fusion on the plate and palette not only creates a cohesive and immersive experience but also fosters a deeper appreciation for the diversity and heritage represented in the culinary offerings.

The transformative power of this cultural fusion lies in its ability to transport diners to different corners of the world without leaving their seats. When the art on the walls resonates with the flavors on the plate, it creates a synergy that elevates the dining experience to a cultural journey. Restaurants recognize that this intentional fusion of culinary and artistic elements not only appeals to the senses but also fosters a sense of global exploration within their dining spaces.

Artful Aftertaste - Extending the Experience Beyond the Last Bite

Conclude our exploration with "Extending the Experience Beyond the Last Bite," the final chapter that emphasizes how restaurants are strategically extending the impact of artful design beyond the culinary experience. The artful ambiance isn't confined to the time spent at the table; it becomes a lasting memory that lingers in the minds of diners. Imagine a restaurant with an art gallery that patrons can explore after their meal or a coffee shop where the artistic elements extend into a cozy reading corner. The artful aftertaste not only ensures that the impact of the dining experience endures but also transforms the restaurant into a space where patrons return not just for the food but for the overall artistic immersion.

The transformative power of extending the experience lies in its ability to create a sense of attachment and loyalty. When patrons can continue their exploration of art even after the last bite, it adds a layer of continuity to the overall experience. Restaurants recognize that this strategic extension ensures that the artistic ambiance becomes synonymous with their brand, creating a unique and memorable identity in the competitive world of gastronomy.

Beyond White Walls: Unleashing Conference Room Creativity with Inspiring Art

Setting the Canvas for Inspired Collaboration

Conference rooms are more than spaces for meetings; they're canvases waiting to be filled with creativity. In this blog post, we'll explore the transformative power of art in conference rooms, delving into how thoughtfully chosen pieces can inspire innovation, enhance productivity, and create an atmosphere that fuels inspired meetings and presentations.

Art as a Catalyst for Creativity

Imagine walking into a conference room adorned with vibrant paintings, sculptures, or even immersive installations. Art has the power to stimulate creativity by providing a visually dynamic environment that sparks inspiration. Active choices of thought-provoking and diverse art can prompt out-of-the-box thinking, encouraging meeting participants to approach challenges from new perspectives.

Engage with local artists or explore the vast world of contemporary art to find pieces that resonate with the ethos of your organization. By actively incorporating art into your conference room, you set the stage for brainstorming sessions and creative discussions. The active infusion of creativity into the physical space not only enhances the overall meeting experience but also fosters a culture of innovation within the team.

Artful Ambiance for Productive Meetings

Conference rooms often serve as hubs for important discussions and decision-making. By actively curating an ambiance through art, businesses can influence the mood and productivity of meetings. Consider the psychological impact of colors – vibrant hues can energize, while muted tones can promote focus and concentration. Actively choosing art that complements the intended meeting atmosphere can enhance communication and collaboration.

Interactive art installations, such as whiteboards or magnetic walls, can also serve practical purposes during presentations. The active integration of functional art elements not only adds a dynamic touch to the conference room but also actively contributes to a more efficient and productive meeting environment.

Art that Tells a Story - Elevating Presentations

A conference room adorned with storytelling art becomes a powerful backdrop for presentations. Actively selecting pieces that align with the narrative of your presentation adds depth and resonance to your message. Whether it's a mural depicting the evolution of your company or thematic pieces that echo your brand values, the active incorporation of storytelling art transforms presentations into memorable and impactful experiences.

Collaborate with artists to create custom pieces that visually communicate the essence of your message. By actively integrating art that tells a story, businesses not only enhance the visual appeal of their presentations but also actively engage and captivate their audience, leaving a lasting impression.

Dynamic Displays for Engaging Meetings

Take your conference room to the next level by incorporating dynamic and interactive displays. These can range from digital screens showcasing rotating art exhibits to projection mapping that transforms the room during presentations. The active integration of dynamic displays not only adds a tech-savvy touch to the conference room but also keeps participants engaged and visually stimulated.

Consider incorporating touch-screen displays that allow for interactive presentations or digital art that evolves throughout the meeting. By actively choosing dynamic displays, businesses create an immersive and forward-thinking meeting space that aligns with the pace of modern innovation.

Fostering Team Identity with Collaborative Art

Art can be a powerful tool for team-building and fostering a sense of identity. Actively involving team members in the creation of collaborative art installations transforms the conference room into a space that reflects the collective spirit of the team. Whether it's a mural, a sculpture, or a rotating art project, the active participation in creating art promotes teamwork and a sense of ownership.

Encourage team members to contribute their ideas and artistic expressions to the collaborative project. By actively fostering a sense of team identity through art, businesses not only create a unique and personalized conference room but also nurture a positive and cohesive team culture that extends beyond the meeting space.

Artful Evolution - Adapting Conference Rooms for Change

In a dynamic business landscape, conference rooms need to be adaptable. The artful evolution of conference room aesthetics involves regularly updating and refreshing the art to align with the evolving goals and identity of the organization. Actively incorporating a plan for the rotation or addition of art ensures that the conference room remains a dynamic and inspiring space, keeping participants engaged and fostering a sense of anticipation.

Consider creating a calendar for art rotations or incorporating seasonal themes that align with the business calendar. By actively planning for the artful evolution of conference rooms, businesses ensure that their meeting spaces remain fresh, inspiring, and reflective of the ever-changing nature of the organization.

In Conclusion: Transforming Meetings into Masterpieces

The conference room is not just a space; it's a canvas waiting to be filled with the brushstrokes of creativity. By actively infusing art into these spaces, businesses elevate the meeting experience, foster innovation, and create an atmosphere that fuels inspired collaboration. From sparking creativity to enhancing presentations and fostering team identity, the artful touch in conference rooms transforms mundane meetings into masterpieces of inspiration.

Contrasting Textures: Mixing Fabrics and Art for Dynamic Decor

Welcome to the world of "Contrasting Textures," where we explore the artful fusion of fabrics and artwork to create dynamic and visually engaging decor. In this blog post, we'll delve into the harmonious relationship between various textures, uncovering the secrets to achieving a stunning and inviting living space. Join us on a journey through six captivating sections, each revealing the magic of blending fabrics and art for an interior that truly captivates the senses.

Texture Tango: The Dance of Fabrics and Art

In "Texture Tango," we embark on a dance of textures, discovering how different fabrics and art forms can harmonize to create a captivating visual experience. Explore the interplay between smooth and rough, soft and coarse, as we delve into the art of balancing contrasting textures. Learn how to select fabrics that complement your artwork, enhancing both the tactile and visual elements of your decor.

Consider pairing a plush velvet sofa with a bold, abstract painting or a textured fabric wall hanging to infuse your space with a sense of luxury and depth. Texture Tango invites you to embrace the beauty of opposites colliding in a dance of visual and tactile delight.

Cozy Canvas: Fabric Art and Warmth

In "Cozy Canvas," we explore the cozy side of contrasting textures by integrating fabric art into your decor. Discover the warmth and comfort that fabric-based artwork brings to your space, creating a snug and inviting atmosphere. From tapestries and woven wall hangings to fabric-covered canvases, this section unveils the diverse world of fabric-based art.

Consider incorporating a large textile wall hanging in warm tones to transform a blank wall into a cozy canvas that evokes a sense of hygge and comfort. Cozy Canvas invites you to envelop your living space in softness, turning your walls into a comforting haven.

Pattern Play: Mixing Textile Patterns with Art

In "Pattern Play," we dive into the world of textile patterns and their harmonious coexistence with various art styles. Explore the art of combining geometric prints, floral motifs, and abstract patterns with complementary artwork to achieve a dynamic and visually stimulating decor. Learn how to balance bold patterns with subtle art and vice versa, creating a layered and sophisticated look.

Consider pairing a vibrant, patterned area rug with a collection of framed artwork in coordinating colors, creating a harmonious interplay of patterns and artistic expression. Pattern Play encourages you to unleash your creativity and experiment with the endless possibilities of pattern and art fusion.

Textile Tapestry: Wall Art Beyond the Canvas

In "Textile Tapestry," we shift our focus to the versatility of fabric as a medium for creating unique wall art beyond traditional canvases. Explore the world of textile tapestries, macramé wall hangings, and fabric sculptures that add a touch of bohemian charm and texture to your living space. Learn how these textile masterpieces can serve as both art and functional decor elements.

Consider incorporating a large macramé wall hanging as a statement piece that introduces texture, movement, and a touch of handmade artistry to your walls. Textile Tapestry invites you to think beyond conventional canvases and embrace the richness of textile-based wall art.

Sensory Symphony: Fabrics and Art for Multisensory Appeal

In "Sensory Symphony," we explore the concept of creating a multisensory experience by combining fabrics and art. Discover how the tactile qualities of textiles enhance the visual appeal of artwork, creating a rich and immersive environment. From soft throw blankets draped over sofas to textured canvases, this section encourages you to consider the sensory impact of your decor choices.

Consider layering different fabrics, such as a plush rug, velvet throw pillows, and a linen wall hanging, to create a symphony of textures that engage both the eyes and the sense of touch. Sensory Symphony invites you to elevate your decor by appealing to multiple senses, fostering a deeper connection to your living space.

DIY Textile Art: Unleashing Your Creative Expression

In "DIY Textile Art," we empower you to unleash your creativity by incorporating handmade textile elements into your decor. Explore simple and exciting DIY projects, from fabric-covered canvases to hand-stitched wall hangings, that allow you to personalize your space with a touch of your artistic flair. This section provides inspiration and step-by-step ideas for creating one-of-a-kind textile art pieces.

Consider organizing a crafting session with friends or family to create personalized fabric art that reflects your unique style and adds a handmade touch to your living space. DIY Textile Art invites you to embark on a creative journey and infuse your decor with a sense of personal connection.

In Conclusion:

As we conclude our exploration of "Contrasting Textures," celebrate the dynamic synergy of fabrics and art in crafting a living space that stimulates the senses and reflects your individual style. Whether you're drawn to the Texture Tango, Cozy Canvas, Pattern Play, Textile Tapestry, Sensory Symphony, or DIY Textile Art, each section unveils a facet of this captivating design trend.

How to Choose the Right Art Prints for Your Office

Imagine:

A woman in her mid-30s sits at a desk in a modern office space. The office is decorated with sleek furniture and minimalistic decor. On the wall behind her, there are several art prints from Art For The Home and Office's collection. The prints feature abstract and contemporary designs in vibrant colors. The woman is looking at a laptop screen, indicating that she is working. The art prints add a pop of color and personality to the otherwise professional and clean office environment.

When it comes to creating a productive and inspiring work environment, the right art prints can make all the difference. They can add a touch of personality, create a focal point, and even boost creativity. If you're looking to enhance your office space with art prints, here are some tips to help you choose the right ones: Consider the Theme and Style: Art For The Home and Office offers a variety of art prints with themes and styles that include abstract, contemporary, and modern.

Think about the overall aesthetic of your office space and choose art prints that complement it. If you have a sleek and minimalistic office, abstract or contemporary prints with vibrant colors can add a pop of personality. On the other hand, if your office has a more traditional or professional look, you may opt for modern prints with clean lines and muted tones.

Think About the Mood: Art has the power to evoke emotions

and set the mood in a space. Consider the atmosphere you want to create in your office. Do you want it to be calm and serene, or energetic and vibrant? Choose art prints that align with the desired mood. For a calming effect, landscapes or abstract prints with soft colors can work well. If you want to create an energetic and inspiring environment, bold and vibrant prints can do the trick.

Size and Placement: Before purchasing art prints, consider the size of your office space and the available wall space. You don't want the prints to overwhelm the room or get lost in a sea of empty walls. Measure the wall space and choose prints that fit proportionally.

Additionally, think about the placement of the prints. Consider placing them at eye level, where they can be easily seen and appreciated. You can also create a gallery wall by grouping multiple prints together for a visually appealing display.

Know Your Audience: Art For The Home and Office's target audience is men and women aged 25 and older in the US and Canada. When choosing art prints for your office, consider the preferences and tastes of your target audience. Think about what would resonate with them and what would make them feel comfortable and inspired in the space.

Quality and Authenticity: Art For The Home and Office specializes in promoting print-on-demand art prints. While they don't sell AI-generated or original artworks, they ensure high-quality prints that are true to the original designs.

When choosing art prints for your office, make sure to select ones that are well-made and will stand the test of time. Look for prints that are printed on archival-quality paper and use fade-resistant inks.

By considering the theme and style, mood, size and placement, audience preferences, and quality of the art prints, you can choose the right ones to enhance your office space. Art For The Home and Office's collection of abstract and contemporary prints in vibrant colors can add a touch of personality and creativity to your professional environment. So go ahead, browse their collection, and find the perfect art prints for your office!

From The Purple House: Your Source for Stunning Art Prints

Are you looking to add a touch of elegance and sophistication to your home or office space? Look no further than FromThePurpleHouse, your go-to online store for stunning art prints.

We specialize in promoting print-on-demand art prints with a wide range of themes and styles, including abstract, contemporary, and modern. Our curated collection is designed to cater to the tastes of men and women aged 25 and older in the US and Canada who appreciate the beauty of art.

Art has the power to transform any space and evoke emotions. It can be a reflection of your personality and style, and at FromThePurpleHouse, we understand the importance of finding the perfect piece to enhance your decor and express your unique taste. That's why we offer a carefully selected collection of high-quality art prints that are sure to impress.

Whether you're looking for a bold and vibrant abstract piece to make a statement, a contemporary print to add a modern touch, or a minimalist design to create a sense of calm, we have something for everyone. Our prints are created by Pictorem using the latest printing technology, ensuring that every detail is captured with precision and clarity. The colors are vibrant and true to life, making our prints a true work of art.

One of the advantages of print-on-demand art prints is that they are customizable. You can choose the size, frame, and even the type of paper to suit your preferences and the specific needs of your space. This allows you to create a truly personalized piece that fits perfectly into your home or office.

At FromThePurpleHouse, we believe that art should be accessible to everyone. That's why we offer competitive prices without compromising on quality. We work with a talented artist to bring you a diverse range of styles and themes, ensuring that there is something for every taste and budget.

Shopping for art prints online can sometimes be overwhelming, but our user-friendly website makes it easy to browse and find the perfect piece. You can search by theme, style, or even color, making it convenient to narrow down your options and find exactly what you're looking for. Our detailed product descriptions and high-resolution images give you a clear idea of what to expect, so you can make an informed decision.

So why wait?

Bring art into your life and transform your space with FromThePurpleHouse. Shop our collection of stunning art prints today and discover the perfect piece to enhance your decor and express your unique style. With our high-quality prints and affordable prices, you can create a beautiful and inspiring space that you'll love coming home to.

The End

Acknowledgement

For **Jodi DiLiberto**— the artist whose vision colors my world.

Your creativity is a reminder that art is not just something we make, but something we *live*. Your courage, your curiosity, and the way you transform emotion into color continue to inspire every page I write.

To anyone holding this book: If you wish to see the heart behind my own creative life, visit Jodi's work at **From the Purple House: www.fromthepurplehouse.art**

Her art is a world of its own—vibrant, intuitive, and deeply human. I'm endlessly grateful to walk beside her.

About The Author

Neil J Milliner

Neil J. Milliner is a contemporary author, creative educator, and publisher focusing on helping creatives, introverts, and musicians build authentic brands, overcome perfectionism, and navigate career challenges through practical, psychology-backed guides. He writes books on music marketing (*The Musician's Marketing Playbook), songwriting (*Emotional Hooks Handbook), sustainable living, self-improvement (*How to Feel Better Without Fixing Everything), and building creative spaces. He runs his own imprint, Books by Neil J, and emphasizes connecting with one's core self for aligned, meaningful creation.

Key Themes in His Work:
- Authenticity: Building brands and creating music that reflects your true self.
- Overcoming Perfectionism: Practical strategies to move past creative blocks and endless tweaking.
- Music Industry Guidance: Marketing, songwriting, and technical advice for musicians.
- Mindful Living: Eco-habits and personal growth for creatives.

Who He Helps:
- Musicians, songwriters, producers
- Creative introverts
- Entrepreneurs and creatives seeking genuine connection

- Individuals wanting to live more sustainably